DISTRACTIONS
FROM DESTINY

by Harry and Cheryl Salem

DISTRACTIONS FROM DESTINY

8 DISTRACTIONS YOU MUST OVERCOME TO ACHIEVE YOUR LIFE'S PURPOSE

by Harry and Cheryl Salem

Harrison House
Tulsa, Oklahoma

05 04 03 02 01   10 9 8 7 6 5 4 3 2 1

Distractions From Destiny—
8 Distractions You Must Overcome To Achieve Your Life's Purpose
ISBN 1-57794-434-8
Copyright © 2001 by Salem Family Ministries
P.O. Box 701287
Tulsa, Oklahoma 74170

Published by Harrison House, Inc.
P.O. Box 35035
Tulsa, Oklahoma 74153

TABLE OF CONTENTS

INTRODUCTION

RESTORED FOR A PURPOSE

BY HARRY AND CHERYL

C an you say without a shadow of any doubt that you are walking in the destiny to which God has called you? Do you have the joy and fulfillment of being in the center of His will for your life and enjoying all the blessings of His provision? If you answered these two questions with a resounding "yes," you have reached a level of spiritual maturity that many believers strive for but rarely attain. The reason so many people don't discover their purpose or reach their full potential is that they are distracted from their destiny. Distractions are a ploy of Satan to steal and destroy our God-given dreams and visions before they become reality. That is why we must be on guard at all times, preventing him from sidetracking us from our destiny.

We know what it is to stand guard against the devil's distractions. When our little six-year-old daughter, Gabrielle Christian Salem, was diagnosed with an inoperable, life-threatening brain tumor in January 1999, we determined in our hearts not to become distracted from ministering to others and spreading the good news of the Gospel. Gabrielle wouldn't allow us to be distracted, because she knew her purpose and never wavered from it. During the year of her illness she sang and ministered in over 100 services, carrying her "Barbie" backpack with the computerized IV pump onto the platform with her. The last time she sang was at Rhema Bible Church in Tulsa. She had been very sick all day. I said, "Honey, I know you don't feel well. We are here as a family, but you don't have to sing tonight. You can just go on home. Mommy and the boys and I will do this."

She looked me in the eye, shook her finger in my face, and said, "Oh, yes, I do. This is *what I do!*" With that, she picked up her backpack, marched out onto the platform, sang her song, went backstage, and threw up. *Then* she went home. She would not allow sickness to distract her from what she was called to do—to minister to people and bring them to Jesus. Many times during that year we followed her lead as she prayed over people in prayer lines or handed out WWJD (What Would Jesus Do?) bracelets to everyone she met and told them about her Jesus. She was unstoppable.

When she graduated to heaven on November 23, 1999, we were devastated. It felt as if a light had gone out in our family, but we recognized a demonic plan to try to distract us from our destiny by breaking our focus. God revealed to our hearts that although we were in mourning, the Son would shine and morning would come again. We knew as believers we were not to mourn as the world mourns, without hope. So we held on to the promise of restoration and focused on the answer—*Jesus*.

As we set our eyes on Jesus, He lovingly restored our lives. There are three important principles that He revealed to us about restoration.

First, He taught us that restoration is not the end; it is a new beginning. When God restores His people, He takes them to a higher level of faith and multiplies their blessings to a greater degree than ever before. When Gabrielle went home to be with Jesus, our faith didn't die; it became stronger.

Second, God showed us that restoration is a process that has a beginning *and* an end. It doesn't go on forever. Each step in the mourning and restoration process lasts only a season. Each one passes. We will never forget who Gabrielle is. However, we aren't remembering how she died; we are remembering how she lived. She will be intertwined in our ministry for life. It still hurts, but we are coming to the end of the intense pain of living without her on this earth. When we get to the end of that season, He will take us further than we have ever been.

Third, *after* restoration comes something supernatural from God: divine visitation. We are not the same people we were before we walked *through* the testing and trial of Gabrielle's illness and home-going. We walked *through* the fire, but we were not burned. God said, *"Now* you've been through something. *Now* I can use you." What you have walked out, walked through, and learned along the path of healing and restoration in your own life prepares you for this visitation.

With divine visitation comes a release to move up to a higher level and go beyond the past season. It is during this time that God will plant a dream in your heart or expand your vision. The Hebrew word for vision means "signifies an agreement."[1] When you embrace the vision God has for your life, you are coming into agreement with God regarding your destiny. You are answering His call to advance His kingdom.

Each and every one of us has a destiny to fulfill in the present and in the future. First, our destiny is to come to Jesus. However, God doesn't restore us just to set us aside. He restores us to fulfill another specific destiny for His kingdom—to bring others to Jesus.

When Gabrielle went home, our priorities changed. Our vision grew wider and higher. Suddenly nothing was important except bringing people to Jesus. At the home-going celebration we prayed for people, imparted the anointing into them, and declared into the heavenlies: "Devil, you will be sorry you started this. We will pull souls into God's kingdom that you just knew would never come in. We will pray for them, stand for them, and speak the Word over them until they come in."

What Satan had meant to use to distract us from our destiny and destroy our ministry, instead more clearly defined our focus. We have seen multitudes in the valley of decision come to Jesus, just as the prophet Joel speaks of in this Scripture:

> *Put in the sickle, for the [vintage] harvest is ripe; come, get down and tread the grapes, for the winepress is full; the*

vats overflow, for the wickedness [of the peoples] is great. Multitudes, multitudes in the valley of decision! For the day of the Lord is near in the valley of decision.

Joel 3:13,14

This is why we are compelled to write this book. Lives are hanging in the balance, waiting for you to find your destiny and lead them out of the valley of decision. We want to share with you the biblical principles that will help you discover and clearly define God's will and purpose for your life. We want to show you how to identify and avoid the distractions the enemy puts in your path to keep you from being all God has created and called you to be. We will share with you a simple three-step distraction-buster formula and specific keys to praying more effectively. By the time you finish this book you will be equipped to define your vision in writing, to deposit vision in others, and to expand your vision while protecting your God-given assets.

When we wander aimlessly through life, Satan gets the glory. However, our God deserves *all* the glory. He has a specific purpose for our lives, and it is for His glory. Now is the time to step up to the plate and do what God has called us to do. We are destined for greatness.

DESTINED FOR GREATNESS

BY HARRY

A re you constantly searching for who you are and what your purpose in life is? Just when you think you have found your niche in life, do you find yourself distracted and moving off in a totally different direction? If so, you aren't alone. This battle has been raging within humanity since the Fall in the Garden of Eden.

God created man in His image, brought him to life with His very breath, and gave him complete authority over the earth for the purpose of serving and glorifying Him.

> *Then the Lord God formed man from the dust of the ground and breathed into his nostrils the breath or spirit of life, and man became a living being.*
>
> **Genesis 2:7**

God said, Let Us [Father, Son, and Holy Spirit] make mankind in Our image, after Our likeness, and let them have complete authority over the fish of the sea, the birds of the air, the [tame] beasts, and over all of the earth, and over everything that creeps upon the earth. So God created man in His own image, in the image and likeness of God He created him; male and female He created them. And God blessed them and said to them, Be fruitful, multiply, and fill the earth, and subdue it [using all its vast resources in the service of God and man]; and have dominion over the fish of the sea, the birds of the air, and over every living creature that moves upon the earth.

Genesis 1:26-28

We can see from these passages that God specifically created humanity to fulfill a great purpose. We are destined for greatness. This truth is almost more than our human minds can comprehend.

However, what happens next in the biblical record of human history explains why so many people struggle to find their purpose and live unfulfilled lives.

THE FIRST IDENTITY CRISIS

Adam and Eve lived in a garden paradise without a worry in the world. They walked and talked with God on a daily basis. Life was perfect. Then along came a crafty, deceitful serpent [Satan] to distract them from their destiny.

Now the serpent was more cunning than any beast of the field which the Lord God had made. And he said to the woman, "Has God indeed said, 'You shall not eat of every tree of the garden'?" And the woman said to the serpent, "We may eat the fruit of the trees of the garden; but of the fruit of the tree which is in the midst of the garden, God has said, 'You shall not eat it, nor shall you touch it, lest you die.'" Then the serpent said to the woman, "You will not surely die. For God knows that in the day you eat of it your eyes will be opened, and you will be like God, knowing good and evil." So when the woman saw that the tree was good for food, that it was pleasant to the eyes, and a tree desirable to make one wise, she took of its fruit and ate. She also gave to her husband with her, and he ate.

Genesis 3:1-6 NKJV

By their own willful disobedience (sin), Adam and Eve suddenly found themselves naked and hiding in shame, pointing their fingers in blame, stripped of their God-given authority over the earth, cut off from their intimate relationship with the Father, and cast out of their beautiful garden into the cold, cruel world to make a living for themselves. What a culture shock that must have been! Talk about an identity crisis! With no clear purpose, not knowing where to go or what to do first, they must have felt frightened, alone, unprepared, and perhaps hopelessly confused.

Do any of these emotions sound familiar? Satan has been using the same tactics of deceit and distraction since the Fall to keep men and women from fulfilling the destiny for which they were created.

ABRAM'S DISTRACTIONS

Even the greatest men and women in the Bible fell prey to such distractions at times. For example, after the death of his eldest son, Terah took his family out of the land of Ur of the Chaldees and headed for the land of Canaan. However, he was distracted from his destiny and settled instead in the city of Haran, where he remained until death.

God then spoke to Terah's son Abram, gave him the promise of blessing, and told him to leave his relatives and his father's house in Haran and go to the land He would show him, which was in Canaan.

Though Abram headed in the right direction, he too was distracted. His concern for his nephew, Lot, distracted him from fulfilling God's directive to leave all of his relatives behind. Abram took Lot with him, and Lot caused all sorts of problems and disruptions along the way.

In one such instance, Abram and Lot's herdsmen were fighting over grazing land and water. Here is what Abram said to Lot:

Let there be no strife, I beg of you, between you and me, or between your herdsmen and my herdsmen, for we are relatives. Is not the whole land before you? Separate yourself, I beg of you, from me. If you take the left hand, then I will go to the right; or if you choose the right hand, then I will go to the left.

Genesis 13:8,9

Lot chose all of "the best" land in the Jordan Valley. It was well watered and green like a garden. To keep peace Abram took what was left, or "the rest." When Abram obeyed God and finally separated from his entire family, including Lot, "the rest" became "the blessed" and "the blessed" was better than "the best"! God spoke this blessing to Abram:

> *Lift up now your eyes and look from the place where you are, northward and southward and eastward and westward; For all the land which you see I will give to you and to your posterity forever. And I will make your descendants like the dust of the earth, so that if a man could count the dust of the earth, then could your descendants also be counted. Arise, walk through the land, the length of it and the breadth of it, for I will give it to you.*

Genesis 13:14-17

We know God had a great destiny in store for Abram, whom He would later name Abraham. We also see that from the beginning of Abram's journey on earth until its end, the devil sent distractions to try to prevent that destiny.

The devil will try to do the same thing to you. The moment God gives you a dream or a vision, be prepared for Satan to slip in some sort of distraction to disrupt you or sidetrack you from fulfilling it.

> **THE MOMENT GOD GIVES YOU A DREAM OR A VISION, BE PREPARED FOR SATAN TO SLIP IN SOME SORT OF DISTRACTION TO DISRUPT YOU OR SIDETRACK YOU FROM FULFILLING IT.**

OUR COMMON PURPOSE

Many people are walking around this earth saying, "Why am I here? What is my purpose? Why was I even born?" Some are saying, "There must be more to life than this. What am I missing?" To gain a better perspective on what our common purpose is, let's look at one of the most visual depictions of destiny in this familiar story of Jesus and Peter walking on the water:

> *And in the fourth watch [between 3:00—6:00 A.M.] of the night, Jesus came to them, walking on the sea. And when the disciples saw Him walking on the sea, they were terrified and said, It is a ghost! And they screamed out with fright. But instantly He spoke to them, saying, Take courage! I AM! Stop being afraid! And Peter answered Him, Lord, if it is You, command me to come to You on the water. He said, Come! So Peter got out of the boat and walked on the water, and he came toward Jesus. But when he perceived and felt the strong wind, he was frightened, and as he began to sink, he cried out, Lord, save me [from death]! Instantly Jesus reached out His hand and caught and held him, saying to him, O you of little faith, why did you doubt? And when they got into the boat, the wind ceased. And those in the boat knelt and worshiped Him, saying, Truly You are the Son of God!*
>
> **Matthew 14:25-33**

When we read this story most of us focus on the fact that Peter walked on water and sank, as if that was such a bad thing. Have you ever stopped to ask yourself what you would have done if you had been in the boat with Peter when Jesus said, "Come"?

Some of us, like the other eleven disciples, would never have even put a toe in the water. Then, instead of saying, "Go, Peter!" we probably would have said, "I can't believe that fool got out of the boat!"

Though he may have stumbled on his journey, Peter actually fulfilled his destiny. Peter's destiny was not to walk on the water. His destiny was the same as yours and mine: to come to Jesus.

CHOOSE TO BE A SURVIVOR!

Peter took the risk to do whatever was necessary to get to Jesus. Peter made a choice that day to be a survivor, a part of the remnant whom the Lord calls, spoken of by the prophet Joel:

> *And whoever shall call on the name of the Lord shall be delivered and saved, for in Mount Zion and in Jerusalem there shall be those who escape, as the Lord has said, and among the remnant [of survivors] shall be those whom the Lord calls.*

Joel 2:32

A survivor is someone who is willing to get in the middle of the battle and endure the blood, sweat, and tears. A survivor refuses to quit or back down from what he believes. A survivor says, "I don't care how it feels, and I don't care if everyone thinks I'm crazy; I'm going to go to Jesus."

Peter was the only one who took the step that no one else would take that day. When Peter got out of the boat, he was so focused on Jesus that he didn't even consider whether it was possible for a human being to walk on water. He simply obeyed: He stepped out of the boat and started walking toward Jesus. Jesus alone was the remnant that day. Peter did what he had to do to become a part of that remnant—to become a survivor.

> **TAKING ACTION IS ESSENTIAL TO LIVING OUT OUR DESTINY. WE WILL NEVER BE ALL WE WERE CREATED TO BE UNTIL WE DO WHAT WE WERE CREATED TO DO.**

Will we be survivors? Will we dare to take a step toward Jesus, our destiny? Or will we be the ones who stay in the boat and criticize the one who does step out? Taking action is essential to living out our destiny. We will never be all we were created to be until we do what we were created to do.

DO WHATEVER IT TAKES

Living with Cheryl is always an adventure. Along our journey we have learned how to do what it takes to fulfill our destiny. Not long after Cheryl underwent colon cancer surgery, she and I decided to drive our motor coach to California with our boys and do some sight-seeing along the way. We visited the Grand Canyon and then headed for Phoenix, Arizona.

Cheryl, who had been carefully monitoring her diet since her surgery, was munching on a protein bar. Suddenly she went berserk.

I almost drove off the road trying to figure out what was causing all the commotion. When she turned to look at me, all I saw was a gaping hole where her front tooth should have been.

She didn't appreciate my humor at all when I said, "Well, they'll know you're the Miss America from the country when they see that toothless smile!"

When she had bitten down into the protein bar, more than half of her front tooth had broken off and stuck in the bar. That was bad enough, but what made it worse was the fact that the next day she had a film shoot in Phoenix for a segment of PAX Network's *It's a Miracle.* The program would reenact the car wreck Cheryl survived at eleven years old and her subsequent miraculous healing.

It was now 5 P.M., and we still had a five-hour drive to Phoenix. The film crew, who had to fly out to another location the next day, had a very limited amount of time to shoot Cheryl's segment. We simply had to be there at 8 A.M. the next morning.

"Miss Toothless" was frantic, but I can always count on Cheryl to come up with a solution. I don't know why I was surprised when she said, "Harry, you've got to find a Wal-Mart!"

"A Wal-Mart? Why do we need a Wal-Mart?"

"You've got to find some superglue. You're going to have to glue my tooth back in."

I dutifully found a Wal-Mart and bought the superglue.

The superglue manufacturers say that all you need is a drop to fix anything. The problem is that they must not have told that to the package designers, because it is impossible to squeeze out just a drop. As I squeezed the tube to put a tiny drop on Cheryl's tooth fragment, the glue came gushing out. Instantly, I had her tooth securely attached to the end of my finger.

As Cheryl reached over and ripped her tooth off my finger, along with a sizeable piece of my skin, she said, "You're not messing up the only part of my tooth I've got. You've got to be more careful."

That was easy for her to say. I reapplied a smaller amount of glue on the tooth, held her head back, and shoved the broken portion of the tooth back onto her remaining front tooth. Examining my handiwork, we discovered that the tooth was crooked and that the thick dab of glue had hardened into a glob on the front of her tooth. It was better than having a gaping hole—but not good enough to be on national television.

By this time Cheryl was digging in her purse, and she came up with an emery board, which she handed to me and said, "You can file off the bottom of the tooth and the extra glue with this."

That little exercise was a sight to behold. This could only have happened to Cheryl. When we finished, it didn't look great, but it was better than no tooth. We arrived in Phoenix at one o'clock in the morning.

Cheryl made it to the television taping on time, and no one noticed her tooth. She was so careful not to touch the tooth with her tongue for fear it would pop out that she talked with a little bit of a lisp, but no one seemed to know the difference.

Many people have told us about seeing that program on PAX Network and being blessed by it. The program about a little crippled girl's healing that led to her reign as Miss America was done for God's glory, and lives are being impacted and changed by it.

We believe this was an appointment with destiny that Satan did his best to sidetrack. Cheryl could have said, "I can't do this with a broken tooth," and perhaps never had the opportunity to complete the taping. Instead, she chose to do whatever it took to fulfill her destiny.

DESTINED FOR A CROWN

In 1980, Cheryl walked the aisle in Atlantic City and was crowned Miss America. More importantly, years before that she walked an aisle and accepted Jesus Christ as her Lord and Savior. Cheryl knew her destiny was to come to Jesus and her purpose was to bring others into His kingdom.

Cheryl's identity is in Christ, not in the Miss America title. However, this title has opened doors she could never have walked through otherwise, and she has used every opportunity to tell the multitudes about Jesus and has touched lives by demonstrating His love wherever she has gone.

She has not done these things for the glittering crown she wore as Miss America. She has done them for the crown that is laid up for her in heaven.

People today still remember her testimony. Cheryl left her mark on the Miss America organization because she refused to compromise her values or her purpose in God's kingdom. They were probably never so glad to see a reign end, but she initiated some significant changes that benefited each future Miss America.

MAKING A MARK

In the fall of 2000, *People Magazine* ran an article featuring all sixty-one surviving Miss Americas. Individuals who read the article and looked at the photos noticed that our family stood out, because our family stands for something— Jesus Christ! His love shines through that picture for the whole world to see. We have a destiny, and we are fulfilling it together. We are not missing the mark of our destiny but making God's mark on this generation.

What does it mean to miss the mark? In 1 John 3:8-9 the Greek root word for sin is *hamartano,* which means "to miss the mark."[1] Let's read this passage inserting the original meaning into it:

> *He who* [misses the mark] *is of the devil, for the devil has* [missed the mark] *from the beginning. For this purpose the Son of God was manifested, that He might destroy the works of the devil. Whoever has been born of God does not* [miss the mark], *for His seed remains in him; and he cannot* [miss the mark], *because he has been born of God.*
>
> **1 John 3:8,9** NKJV

Missing the mark is more than just being distracted from your destiny. When we are walking in the light of God and we hear Jesus say, "You missed the mark," we are walking in sin.

When we allow sin to distract our focus from God's purpose, we are unable to aim properly at the mark of our destiny. A bow and arrow illustrate this point well. If an archer does not align his eyes and body properly toward his goal, his arrow will miss the mark. Likewise, if our focus is not aligned properly toward our goal in Christ, we will miss the mark of His destiny. Paul spoke of this goal in his letter to the Philippians:

> *Brethren, I do not count myself to have apprehended; but one thing I do, forgetting those things which are behind and reaching forward to those things which are ahead, I press toward the goal for the prize of the upward call of God in Christ Jesus.*

> **Philippians 3:13,14 NKJV**

The "goal" Paul is speaking of is the "mark." Here again, "missing the mark" is sinning. If we want to hit, not miss, the mark, or fulfill our destiny (upward call) in Christ, we cannot continue in sin or even look behind at our past failures or successes. We must look forward and reach toward our Lord, who is our destiny.

LIFT JESUS HIGHER

You will have many opportunities to hit the mark throughout your life. Watch for them and seize them. God will open doors for you and take you into the wonderful places where He has called you. It is when you get to those places that you have to make a decision on the spot whom you will give the glory to and lift up.

Right now you may say, "Every chance I get I'll give God the glory." But the moment you are in the face of God's victory is the moment you have to know who you are inside and why you are who you are. You have to know in your "knower" that God has put you on this earth for His destiny and His purpose.

> YOU HAVE TO KNOW IN YOUR "KNOWER" THAT GOD HAS PUT YOU ON THIS EARTH FOR HIS DESTINY AND HIS PURPOSE.

But arise and stand upon your feet; for I have appeared to you for this purpose, that I might appoint you to serve as [My] minister and to bear witness both to what you have seen of Me and to that in which I will appear to you.

Acts 26:16

God has great things for you to accomplish, but you will have to choose every day who will get the glory for what you do. Will you be silent about whom you love, or will you proclaim Him as Lord and shout it from the rooftops?

You don't have to be obnoxiously zealous, but if you lift up the Father and make it known throughout the world that you are not ashamed of Him, then He won't be ashamed of you. He will always be there for you. All He asks is that you do your part to obey His Word and give Him the glory.

DO NOT FEAR MAN

Don't let the fear of man discourage you from lifting up the name of Jesus and coming to Him. Moses fought this battle of fear with the children of Israel more than once and had to remind them of the consequences of being discouragers instead of encouragers, as recorded in this passage:

> *Why do you discourage the hearts of the Israelites from going over into the land which the Lord has given them?*

Thus your fathers did when I sent them from Kadesh-barnea to see the land!

Numbers 32:7,8

The Israelites had just destroyed the Midianites and taken their riches. The sons of Gad and Reuben then looked at the land of the Midianites on the east side of the Jordan and were prepared to accept what looked best rather than go over the Jordan into the Promised Land and be blessed. Moses reminded them what happened to their forefathers, who came out of Egypt and died wandering in the wilderness for forty years because of the sin of unbelief that spread through the camp when the people became distracted by fear and discouragement. Instead of giving God the glory for what He had done in defeating the Midianites and for what He was prepared to do in giving them the Promised Land, these Israelites were about to turn their backs on God again.

However, this time they listened to Moses and did what God told them to do. Armed for battle, they crossed over the Jordan and subdued the land because God was with them. Then the sons of Gad and Reuben were rewarded with their inheritance, the land on the east side of the Jordan, because they had been obedient and given God the glory.

GET OUT OF THE CLOSET

It is time for us to become armed for battle and to subdue the land that God has given us. In other words, it is time for us to get out of the closet of fear, sin, or whatever is holding us back, and to fulfill our destiny. God isn't looking for closet

Christians, ones who are stuck in closets of distraction. In Revelation 3, he describes such people as "lukewarm," and shows us His nauseated opinion of them:

"I know your works, that you are neither cold nor hot. I could wish you were cold or hot. So then, because you are lukewarm, and neither cold nor hot, I will vomit you out of My mouth."

Revelation 3:15,16 NKJV

In the following passage, God shows us further how he feels about those who are called but do not press toward their destiny, or "bear fruit":

Every tree that does not bear good fruit is cut down and cast into the fire. Therefore, you will fully know them by their fruits. Not everyone who says to Me, Lord, Lord, will enter the kingdom of heaven, but he who does the will of My Father Who is in heaven. Many will say to Me on that day, Lord, Lord, have we not prophesied in Your name and driven out demons in Your name and done many mighty works in Your name? And then I will say to them openly (publicly), I never knew you; depart from Me, you who act wickedly [disregarding My commands].

Matthew 7:19-23

If you came face to face with Jesus today, would He say to you, "Well done, My good and faithful servant," or would He say, "I never knew you; depart from Me"?

Today is the day to choose which master you will serve—God or man. Your destiny is defined by who you are and why you are doing what you are doing. If you aren't living for God's glory, then you are serving the wrong master—Satan. There is

no middle ground. You can't straddle
the fence.

JESUS WON THE BATTLE

The battle over our identity as
sons and daughters of a loving Father
began in the Garden of Eden. God
knew before Creation what would
happen in the Garden, and He had a
plan already in place. He sent His

> **YOUR DESTINY
> IS DEFINED BY
> WHO YOU ARE AND
> WHY YOU ARE
> DOING WHAT
> YOU ARE DOING.**

only Son to earth to walk among men as a living witness of His
love, to shed His blood and die for the sins of all men, and to be
raised from the dead to live and reign once again in heavenly
places. As the following Scripture passage shows, with the shed-
ding of Jesus' blood, we were adopted into the family of God and
destined for greatness:

> *Even as [in His love] He chose us [actually picked us out
> for Himself as His own] in Christ before the foundation of
> the world, that we should be holy (consecrated and set apart
> for Him) and blameless in His sight, even above reproach,
> before Him in love. For He foreordained us (destined us,
> planned in love for us) to be adopted (revealed) as His own
> children through Jesus Christ, in accordance with the
> purpose of His will [because it pleased Him and was His
> kind intent]—[So that we might be] to the praise and the
> commendation of His glorious grace (favor and mercy),
> which He so freely bestowed on us in the Beloved. In Him
> we have redemption (deliverance and salvation) through
> His blood, the remission (forgiveness) of our offenses
> (shortcomings and trespasses), in accordance with the*

riches and the generosity of His gracious favor, which He lavished upon us in every kind of wisdom and understanding (practical insight and prudence.)

Ephesians 1:4-8

Adam and Eve had lost their authority over the earth, intimacy with the Father, and godly heritage when they ate from the Tree of the Knowledge of Good and Evil. However, Jesus reclaimed all these assets through His death and resurrection.

In Him we also were made [God's] heritage (portion) and we obtained an inheritance; for we had been foreordained (chosen and appointed beforehand) in accordance with His purpose, Who works out everything in agreement with the counsel and design of His [own] will, so that we who first hoped in Christ [who first put our confidence in Him have been destined and appointed to] live for the praise of His glory!

Ephesians 1:11,12

ENFORCE THE VICTORY

How much clearer could it be that we have a destiny that is greater than anything this world has to offer? Jesus triumphed over Satan, and the war over our identity and sonship has already been won.

Why is it that we still struggle with our identity and purpose in life and find it so difficult to believe that God loves us?

The problem is that we fail to enforce that victory here on earth and keep giving ground to the enemy in the realm of our souls, which are made up of our minds, wills, and emotions.

The soul is where the battle is most intense. The mind is the place in which the devil infiltrates our defenses with his lies and accusations to distract us from the truth of what the Word of God says. He knows that the mind set on the flesh is death, but the mind set on the Spirit is life and peace.

Therefore, we must take every thought captive and bring every thought into obedience to the Word. (2 Cor. 10:5.) This is the only way we will overcome broken focus, the number one distraction that keeps us from reaching our full potential in Christ.

DESTINY KEYS:

1. Examine your heart and ask the Lord to reveal to you any lies or deceptions that have prevented you from receiving His love and acceptance.

2. Find a Scripture that counters each lie; then read that Scripture out loud each day, personalizing it, until your heart is changed and at peace. Use a Bible version that is easy to understand.

   Example:

   The deception is that you are unworthy of His love. Personalizing a Scripture in *The Living Bible* to counter this lie, you might say:

   Long ago, even before he made the world, God chose [me] *to be his very own, through what Christ would do for* [me]; *he decided then to make* [me] *holy in his eyes, without a single fault—*[I stand] *before him covered with his love. His unchanging plan has always been to adopt* [me] *into his own family by sending Jesus Christ to die for* [me]. *And he did this because he wanted to!*

Ephesians 1:4,5 TLB

DISTRACTION 1:
BROKEN FOCUS

BY HARRY

D id you know that failure is nothing more than broken focus? What causes us to break our focus? Going back to the story of Jesus and Peter walking on the water, we can see that Peter did two things that caused him to break his focus. He began to think (he perceived) and to feel. As he became more moved by what he was thinking and feeling than by what he was doing, he lost his focus and began to sink. He took his eyes off His source and began to fail.

Thoughts and feelings will distract you in the blink of an eye. That is why it is so critical to focus on Jesus and not on what you think or how you feel. The way you think or feel may cause you to forget what you are supposed to be focused on or may even be contrary to what God wants to do in your life.

Satan won't give up until the last battle is fought. He won't admit that his defeat is already sealed by Jesus' victory over death. He is afraid of our destiny because he knows that whatever we do for the kingdom of God puts one more nail in his coffin. That's why the closer we get in time to that final battle the more intense the warfare becomes.

THE BATTLE FOR YOUR MIND

Satan's first line of attack is against our minds with lies, condemnation, accusations, and temptations. He found a strategy that worked in the Garden of Eden, and he has been using it ever since. He even tried it on Jesus in the wilderness right after He was baptized.

> *Then Jesus, full of and controlled by the Holy Spirit, returned from the Jordan and was led in [by] the [Holy] Spirit for (during) forty days in the wilderness (desert), where He was tempted (tried, tested exceedingly) by the devil. And He ate nothing during those days, and when they were completed, He was hungry. Then the devil said to Him, If You are the Son of God, order this stone to turn into a loaf [of bread]. And Jesus replied to him, It is written, Man shall not live and be sustained by (on) bread alone but by every word and expression of God.*
>
> Luke 4:1-4

If Satan challenged Jesus, the Son of God, to a battle for His mind, then who are we to think he won't challenge us as sons and daughters of God? No one is exempt from such warfare.

JESUS IS THE PATTERN

To learn how to overcome the attacks on our minds that are meant to break our focus and distract us from our destiny, we must look at what Jesus did and follow His example. Here are the steps He took:

1. He was baptized in water *and* in the Spirit.

2. He submitted to the authority of the Father because He knew the testing was for His good to prepare Him for what was to come in His ministry.

3. He was full of and controlled by the Spirit. The Spirit was a key to His power to remain focused in the face of tests and trials.

4. He fasted and denied His flesh in the face of temptation. He didn't allow his feelings of hunger to distract Him from His purpose.

5. To prove He was the Son of God, He ignored the devil's taunting words rather than dialoguing with him. (The first mistake Eve made was to talk with the serpent. That was how she got hooked.)

6. He spoke in the power and the authority of the Word of God.

> JESUS KNEW THAT IT IS IN TIMES OF TESTS AND TRIALS THAT WE LEARN TO LIVE BY THE WORD OF GOD.

Jesus knew that it is in times of tests and trials that we learn to live by the Word of God. He demonstrated for us how to stand against the enemy and live victoriously. To do that we must have the Word inside of us before the battle comes, and we must believe and do what it says.

In our family, we speak and pray the Word of God over each other every day. We taught our children how to do this from the time they learned to talk. We could never have walked through the test and the trial of Gabrielle's illness and home-going if we hadn't deposited that Word inside us in advance. When the evil report hit us so suddenly and unexpectedly, we could not have maintained our focus if we had been scrambling to find the right Scriptures to pray. Gabrielle knew how to speak the pure Word of God over herself, and so did the boys. Yes, we continued to search the Scriptures for new revelation, but we had a firm foundation already implanted in our spirits. The Word flowed out of our hearts and minds because it had been deposited and nurtured over a period of several years.

> **THE WORD IS OUR PRIMARY WEAPON IN THE BATTLEFIELD OF OUR MINDS.**

USE YOUR SPIRITUAL WEAPONS

The Word is our primary weapon in the battlefield of our minds. The apostle Paul wrote that it is a spiritual battle we face and that we must use spiritual weapons:

> *For though we walk in the flesh, we do not war according to the flesh. For the weapons of our warfare are not carnal but mighty in God for pulling down strongholds, casting down arguments and every high thing that exalts itself*

against the knowledge of God, bringing every thought into captivity to the obedience of Christ.

2 Corinthians 10:3-5 NKJV

This Scripture is clear. It tells us we are to bring "every thought into captivity to the obedience of Christ." In other words, when we start struggling with circumstances in our lives, it is time to examine whether what we are thinking lines up with the Word of God. If it doesn't, we had better refocus our thoughts before we fall into one of the enemy's traps and end up in serious trouble.

THE PRICE OF DISOBEDIENCE

Everyone is susceptible to such distractions. King David was a mighty man of war as well as a psalmist. He had a heart after God and wrote some of the most powerful and beautiful songs of praise and thanksgiving ever recorded. Yet even he fell prey to the distractions of the enemy when he allowed his focus to be broken. It could have cost him his kingdom, and he paid a terrible price for his sin. His story is recorded in the Scriptures so we can learn from it:

In the spring, when kings go forth to battle, David sent Joab with his servants and all Israel, and they ravaged the Ammonites [country] and besieged Rabbah. But David remained in Jerusalem.

2 Samuel 11:1

First, we see that David did not go out with his army as was expected of the king. He remained in Jerusalem while his men were fighting and dying on behalf of the kingdom he ruled. He was in the wrong place at the wrong time and, therefore, had idle time on his hands.

> *One evening David arose from his couch and was walking on the roof of the king's house, when from there he saw a woman bathing; and she was very lovely to behold.*
>
> **2 Samuel 11:2**

We know the rest of the story. David sent for Bathsheba and brought her into his bed. When she became pregnant, David tried to cover up his sin and called her husband, Uriah, back from the war so he would sleep with his wife and think the baby was his own child. Uriah was such a righteous man that he refused to go to his wife when the other men were fighting and living in such difficult conditions. David tried to trick Uriah by getting him drunk, but still Uriah did not go to his wife. David's sin kept compounding, and finally he sent Uriah back to the battlefield with instructions that ensured his death. Now David's spirit not only bore the stain of adultery but also of murder.

David then took Bathsheba as his wife, and she had a son. God was not pleased with all the evil David had done, so He sent the prophet Nathan to speak truth to David. He reminded David of all the ways in which the Lord had blessed him and then told him the price he would pay for his sin.

> *Why have you despised the commandment of the Lord, doing evil in His sight? You have slain Uriah the Hittite with the sword and have taken his wife to be your wife. You have murdered him with the sword of the Ammonites. Now, therefore, the sword shall never depart from your house, because [you have not only despised my command, but] you*

have despised Me and have taken the wife of Uriah the Hittite to be your wife. Thus says the Lord, Behold, I will raise up evil against you out of your own house; and I will take your wives before your eyes and give them to your neighbor, and he shall lie with your wives in the sight of this sun. For you did it secretly, but I will do this thing before all Israel and before the sun. And David said to Nathan, I have sinned against the Lord. And Nathan said to David, The Lord also has put away your sin; you shall not die. Nevertheless, because by this deed you have utterly scorned the Lord and given great occasion to the enemies of the Lord to blaspheme, the child that is born to you shall surely die.

2 Samuel 12:9-14

It is the truth of God's Word that sets us free. David had to have known he was in sin, but it took Nathan's coming and speaking God's Word to him directly to bring conviction and repentance.

When David repented of his sin, God spared his life, but from then on David's household was torn with strife and turmoil. The baby did die, but the second son born to David and Bathsheba was Solomon, whom the Lord loved, who became king following David's death, and who ruled with great wisdom.

The Lord continued to bless David because he repented of his sin, but David's children caused him great pain for the remainder of his

> **THOUGHTS AND EMOTIONS ARE POWERFUL FORCES THAT CAN EASILY BREAK OUR FOCUS AND DISTRACT US FROM OUR DESTINY.**

days. His son Absalom killed his own brother, rebelled against his father, and caused the people to rise up against David. Absalom died in the ensuing battle, in which David's loyal army fought to regain control of the kingdom. While David was on his deathbed, another son, Adonijah, unsuccessfully tried to take his throne. Even his son King Solomon disobeyed God and fell into sin. David sowed bad seed when he allowed his mental and emotional focus to be broken, and he reaped the consequences for the rest of his life.

Thoughts and emotions are powerful forces that can easily break our focus and distract us from our destiny. In recent years we have seen many anointed men and women of God sidetracked from receiving God's best by such distractions as David faced. Some, like David, have repented and are still being used by God. Others have lost their ministries, families, and some even their lives.

NEVER TOO CLOSE TO FAIL

No matter how close we think we are to Jesus, we can still fail. When Peter got out of the boat, he walked all the way to Jesus before he began to sink. How do we know that? Matthew 14:31 says, "Jesus reached out his hand and caught and held him," so he must have been no more than an arm's length away.

> NO MATTER HOW CLOSE WE THINK WE ARE TO JESUS, WE CAN STILL FAIL.

We should never become so prideful that we think, *Oh, I'm so close to Jesus that I could never fail. I will never get my focus off Him.*

Everyone misses the mark sometime. Romans 3:23 says, *"All have sinned...."* The important point to remember is that if we fail, Jesus is right there to pick us up or pull us out if we just call out to Him, as Peter did.

Even David, who was so intimately close to God's heart, failed. He paid dearly for allowing his focus to be broken and warned Solomon not to make the same mistake.

Let your eyes look straight ahead, fix your gaze directly before you. Make level paths your feet and take only ways that are firm. Do not swerve to the right or to the left; keep your foot from evil.

Proverbs 4:25-27 NIV

SET YOUR EYES ON JESUS

If we take these words of wisdom to heart, we will not be distracted. What we see with our eyes is where our mental focus is maintained and where our physical journey will lead. When Peter took his eyes off Jesus and looked at the waves of the storm, his mind focused on thoughts of sinking and his body began to sink. When David let his eyes wander to another man's wife, his mental focus became lust and self-gratification and his flesh followed after it.

This is what God says about the focus of our eyes, our minds, and our flesh:

> *For all that is in the world—the lust of the flesh [craving for sensual gratification] and the lust of the eyes [greedy longings of the mind] and the pride of life [assurance in one's own resources or in the stability of earthly things]—these do not come from the Father but are from the world [itself].*
>
> **1 John 2:16**

What are your eyes most often focused upon? Are you watching TV shows and movies that are filled with sexual innuendoes or blood and violence, or do you carefully screen what you and your family watch? Are you spending hours and hours surfing the Net and participating in chat rooms that discuss subjects that don't glorify the Lord? What sort of music or radio talk shows do you listen to on the way to work? How much time do you spend reading the Bible in comparison to the time you spend reading the newspaper each day?

GOD'S WORD WARNS US REPEATEDLY ABOUT WHAT WE ALLOW OUR EYES TO FOCUS UPON, BECAUSE WHAT WE SEE IS WHAT WE WILL GET.

The answers to these questions will quickly tell you what you are focused on and perhaps why you are not living out your destiny in peace and joy.

You have probably heard this statement used in jest: "What you see is what you get." But there is actually great truth in it. When our eyes are upon the Lord, He will protect us and help us stay focused on our destiny in Him.

> *My eyes are ever toward the Lord, For He shall pluck my feet out of the net.*
>
> **Psalm 25:15 NKJV**

God's Word warns us repeatedly about what we allow our eyes to focus upon, because what we see is what we will get. Here are two such Scriptures:

A discerning man keeps wisdom in view, but a fool's eyes wander to the ends of the earth.

Proverbs 17:24 NIV

"The lamp of the body is the eye. If therefore your eye is good, your whole body will be full of light. But if your eye is bad, your whole body will be full of darkness. If therefore the light that is in you is darkness, how great is that darkness!"

Matthew 6:22,23 NKJV

You may be asking, "How can I guard against broken focus?" The best way is to follow these steps:

1. Establish your life on the foundation of the Word of God by making daily deposits of the Word into you and your family and then believing and doing what it says.

2. Keep your eyes focused on Jesus and His ways, looking straight ahead toward the vision He gives to you.

3. Carefully consider where you are walking so that you will be in the place you have been called to be and not wander into enemy territory, where evil and temptation are lurking.

4. Be filled with the Spirit and led by the Spirit in all that you do.

5. Take every thought captive *before* it gains a foothold in your mind, and renew your mind by speaking the Word of God over every circumstance.

6. Make a daily choice not to allow thoughts and feelings to control your actions by carefully considering whether they line up with the Word.

7. Remain humble and submit yourself to the authority of the Father and His Word, knowing that He loves you.

8. Repent quickly when you sin, and call out to Jesus to pick you up and help you get refocused on Him immediately.

If you faithfully apply these steps to your life, broken focus will no longer be able to distract you from being all that God has called you to be. Now let's keep moving forward and attack the next distraction the enemy uses against us: people.

DESTINY KEYS:

1. Identify two or three past situations in which you experienced failure or disappointment because of broken focus.

2. List specifically what caused you to lose your focus.

3. Write out specific steps you will take to prevent such distractions in the future.

4. Pray this personalized Scripture out loud over yourself for the next seven days, or until you believe it in your heart:

...glorious Father...give [me] *wisdom to see clearly and really understand who Christ is and all that he has done for* [me]. *I pray that* [my heart] *will be flooded with light so that* [I] *can see something of the future he has called* [me] *to share. I want...to realize that God has been made rich because* [I who am] *Christ's have been given to him!* [I] *pray that* [I] *will begin to understand how incredibly great his power is to help those who believe him.*

Ephesians 1:17-19 TLB

DISTRACTION 2:
PEOPLE

BY CHERYL

D anny, a young man with a heart for God, is finishing
pre-med at a prestigious university. He is excited about
medical school and has been accepted in the program
that was his first choice. After completing his medical training,
he wants to dedicate his life to mission work. While providing
medical care to multitudes of people in different countries
around the world and demonstrating the Father's love to those
he helps, he hopes to be a light in the darkness and bring many
into God's kingdom.

Homecoming weekend is approaching, and Julie, one of the
cutest, most popular young women on campus, has agreed to go
to the Homecoming activities with him. She has been his lab
partner in microbiology and is always a lot of fun. Danny hasn't

dated much because of his academic workload, so he is excited about this weekend.

Saturday night arrives, and when Julie comes down the stairs in her black strapless gown, her beauty is breathtaking. Danny gives her a gorgeous corsage of red roses, and she floats out the door on his arm. This will be a night to remember...

Indeed, this night changes Danny's life forever. He eventually falls in love with this beautiful woman who loves the idea of marrying a doctor. What he doesn't know is that she will never share his vision for mission work. Danny and Julie marry the following summer. Gradually she convinces him that a lucrative orthopedic practice in Boston is much more to her liking than the dust and dirt of Africa or India. In fact, she makes it quite clear that she has married a doctor, *not* a missionary.

One evening in the company of the wrong person distracted Danny from his destiny. Is Julie a bad person? Not necessarily, but she has a different vision than Danny and ultimately has stolen his dream to heal bodies and souls on the mission field.

> **THE QUICKEST WAY TO BE DISTRACTED FROM YOUR DESTINY IS TO GET INTO RELATIONSHIP WITH A DREAM STEALER.**

There are two kinds of people in life: dream seekers and dream stealers. A dream seeker will agree with what you are called to do and encourage you along the way. A dream stealer will try to talk you out of it and find ways to break your focus. The quickest way to be distracted from your destiny is to get into relationship with a dream stealer.

BE EQUALLY YOKED

When God instructed us not to be unequally yoked, He wasn't just commanding a believer not to marry an unbeliever. He was also commanding a believer not to marry another believer who will steal his dream. Two believers who don't share the same dream and destiny can destroy each other's dream and never find the peace and joy God meant for them to have. This is often the reason for strife and turmoil in marriages and frequently results in divorce, unless the two people get on the same page and start working in tandem.

> TWO BELIEVERS WHO DON'T SHARE THE SAME DREAM AND DESTINY CAN DESTROY EACH OTHER'S DREAM AND NEVER FIND THE PEACE AND JOY GOD MEANT FOR THEM TO HAVE.

Harry and I were perfect examples of this in the early years of our marriage. We both loved the Lord and knew we were destined to serve Him, but we were coming at it from opposite ends of the spectrum. The old saying, "opposites attract," fit us perfectly. Harry sees everything in black and white with no shades of gray. I'm so spiritually minded that earthly matters don't even enter the picture most of the time.

Harry knew he was marrying a former Miss America who was on a mission for God, but he had no concept what that would mean. Harry wanted a wife who would be at home to cook the meals, rear godly, perfectly behaved children, and, of course, quietly submit to his authority.

I wanted to be a godly wife and a "supermom" and continue with *my* ministry. I was convinced I could do it *all,* even if it killed me, which it almost did. As for being quiet, such a prospect was impossible for my personality to comprehend. Despite my outward act of submission, rebellion brewed deep within my heart. After all, God's call was on my life to preach and to teach and I couldn't give that up. We loved each other and knew God had put us together, but those first few years of marriage were a battleground of conflict that prevented us from focusing on and fulfilling the destiny God had for our family.

Our books *An Angel's Touch* and *Being #1 at Being #2* tell our story of how God changed our hearts and taught us to submit to God and to each other so that He could bring forth Salem Family Ministries.

When we married, we had both been working for God and continued to do so. Ever since being crowned Miss America I had traveled and ministered the Gospel in churches and women's conferences. Harry used his gift of administration behind the scenes with Oral Roberts' ministry and at Oral Roberts University.

Though we were working for God separately, we had no peace until we came to grips with the fact that God wanted us to serve Him together. Furthermore, He didn't want us working *for* Him; He wanted us working *with* Him.

I had always wanted Harry to join me in ministry, but I had to wait until he heard the call himself. The vision God gave us to minister as a family took us out of our comfort zones and honestly upset some people who were closest to us. They were well meaning, loving people, but they hadn't heard the call from God that Harry and I had heard. If Harry had stayed at ORU we would have failed to find our destiny together!

GOD'S DESTINY FULFILLED

Do you remember the story in Genesis of Jacob and Esau? Isaac and Rebekah had been married for twenty years when God answered Isaac's prayer and opened Rebekah's barren womb. She was pregnant with twins, and they caused quite a ruckus in her womb. She asked the Lord what it was all about, and He said:

> *[The founders of] two nations are in your womb, and the separation of two peoples has begun in your body; the one people shall be stronger than the other, and the elder shall serve the younger.*

Genesis 25:23

In the Jewish culture, the eldest son had certain rights as the firstborn and received the father's blessing. The eldest son inherited the father's estate and managed the family's business. Therefore, the Lord's word to Rebekah was unusual in that the elder normally did not serve the younger.

God remembered the promise He had made to Abraham regarding his descendants, and Isaac's sons had an important role to play in fulfilling God's destiny. God knew that Esau, the firstborn of the twins, would not have the strength of character needed to lead His people and would not keep the bloodline pure. Therefore, He had another plan already prepared. Jacob would carry on the pure lineage of the Jewish people and, more importantly, of the Messiah. Thus, God's promise to Abraham would be fulfilled.

Esau was an outdoorsman and a skilled hunter. Today he probably would have been competing in the Olympic decathlon events.

Jacob was not the athletic, outdoor type at all. He was quiet and unassuming. If he were alive today, he might be what is known as a "techie," knowing all there is to know about the latest computer hardware and software and spending his days and nights glued to his computer.

As often happens in families today when the father's favorite son is the star athlete, Isaac was partial to Esau and didn't give Jacob much thought. However, as the old saying goes, still waters run deep. Jacob didn't draw attention to himself, but he was nobody's fool.

Esau had a big ego and wanted what he wanted when he wanted it. Instant gratification was more important than considering the value and importance of his destiny.

Jacob was boiling pottage (lentil stew) one day, when Esau came from the field and was faint [with hunger]. And Esau said to Jacob, I beg of you, let me have some of that red lentil stew to eat, for I am faint and famished! That is why his name was called Edom [red]. Jacob answered, Then sell me today your birthright (the rights of a firstborn). Esau said, See here, I am at the point of death; what good can this birthright do me? Jacob said, Swear to me today [that you are selling it to me]; and he swore to Jacob and sold him his birthright. Then Jacob gave Esau bread and stew of lentils, and he ate and drank

and rose up and went his way. Thus Esau scorned his
birthright as beneath his notice.

Genesis 25:29-34

Another indication of Esau's total disregard for his heritage
and birthright that gave his parents great pain arose years later
when he chose to marry two Hittite women.

Now Esau was 40 years old when he took as wife Judith
the daughter of Beeri the Hittite, and Basemath the
daughter of Elon the Hittite. And they made life bitter and
a grief of mind and spirit for Isaac and Rebekah [their
parents-in-law].

Genesis 26:34,35

Rebekah remembered the prophetic word the Lord had
given her prior to the birth of her sons, and she loved Jacob
most of all. When Isaac was old and ready to give his blessing
to Esau as his firstborn, she and Jacob deceived Isaac. After
dressing Jacob in Esau's clothes and putting animal skins on his
hands and neck to make him hairy like Esau, they entered the
dying man's room. Isaac subsequently gave his blessing to
Jacob instead of Esau.

Isaac was distraught when he learned of Jacob's deception
but could not undo what had already been done. Once the
blessing was given it could not be taken back. Here is what
Isaac said to Esau (a further confirmation of the Lord's word to
Rebekah before the birth of her twins):

Behold, I have made [Jacob] your lord and master; I have
given all his brethren to him for servants, and with corn

and [new] wine have I sustained him. What then can I do for you, my son?

Your [blessing and] dwelling shall all come from the fruitfulness of the earth and from the dew of the heavens above; by your sword you shall live and serve your brother. But [the time shall come] when you will grow restive and break loose, and you shall tear his yoke from off your neck.

Genesis 27:37,39,40

Esau was so furious when he discovered that his brother had stolen his blessing that he vowed to kill Jacob once their father was dead. Rebekah heard of his threat and told Jacob he should leave the country and go to her family until Esau had time to get over his anger. She went to Isaac and convinced him it was best for Jacob to go find a wife among their own people in Haran. Isaac sent Jacob with his blessing to find a wife in the household of Rebekah's brother Laban, saying:

Arise, go to Padan-aram, to the house of Bethuel your mother's father, and take from there as a wife one of the daughters of Laban your mother's brother. May God Almighty bless you and make you fruitful and multiply you until you become a group of peoples. May He give the blessing [He gave to] Abraham to you and your descendants with you, that you may inherit the land he gave to Abraham, in which you are a sojourner.

Genesis 28:2-4

Jacob was a grown man at this time, but he obeyed his parents without any argument or question. While he was on his journey, the Lord gave him a dream that clearly confirmed his destiny. It was the same blessing He had promised Abraham and which his father, Isaac, had spoken over him. It is exciting when God speaks to us of His purpose and destiny, as He did here to Jacob:

> *And he dreamed that there was a ladder set up on the earth, and the top of it reached to heaven; and the angels of God were ascending and descending on it! And behold, the Lord stood over and beside him and said, I am the Lord, the God of Abraham your father [forefather] and the God of Isaac; I will give to you and to your descendants the land on which you are lying. And your offspring shall be as [countless as] the dust or sand of the ground, and you shall spread abroad to the west and the east and the north and the south; and by you and your Offspring shall all the families of the earth be blessed and bless themselves. And behold, I am with you and will keep (watch over you with care, take notice of) you wherever you may go, and I will bring you back to this land; for I will not leave you until I have done all of which I have told you.*

> **Genesis 28:12-15**

HEIRS OF THE COVENANT

Did you know that God gave us the same promise as He gave to Abraham and then to Jacob? Our destiny is just as awesome and powerful today as the day it was spoken thousands of years ago.

> *You are the descendants (sons) of the prophets and the heirs of the covenant which God made and gave to your forefathers, saying to Abraham, And in your Seed (Heir) shall all the families of the earth be blessed and benefited. It was to you first that God sent His Servant and Son Jesus,*

43

when He raised Him up [provided and gave Him for us], to bless you in turning every one of you from your wicked and evil ways.

Acts 3:25,26

And the Scripture, foreseeing that God would justify (declare righteous, put in right standing with Himself) the Gentiles in consequence of faith, proclaimed the Gospel [foretelling the glad tidings of a Savior long beforehand] to Abraham in the promise, saying, In you shall all the nations [of the earth] be blessed.

Now the promises (covenants, agreements) were decreed and made to Abraham and his Seed (his Offspring, his Heir). He [God] does not say, And to seeds (descendants, heirs), as if referring to many persons, but, And to your Seed (your Descendant, your Heir), obviously referring to one individual, Who is [none other than] Christ (the Messiah).

Galatians 3:8,16

> **THROUGH CHRIST YOU HAVE EVERY BLESSING AND PROVISION PROMISED TO ABRAHAM.**

You are an heir of Christ and, therefore, a descendant of His Seed. Through Christ you have every blessing and provision promised to Abraham. God will never leave you or forsake you. That is part of his promise in fulfilling your destiny. He has promised to do all He says He will in and for you.

Focus on Him so you can continue on the journey He has planned for you. God and you are the only ones who know what your destiny is and can see that specific destiny fulfilled.

A TIME AND A SEASON

Harry loved what he did for the Robertses and was good at what he did. There was a time when Harry would not have been willing to walk away from that role, but God plants us in certain places for a season. (As you will recall, He planted Jacob in Laban's household for a season.)

Harry hated having me travel and be away from the family, and yet he knew I had a calling to preach and teach. He never saw himself in such a role, but when God began to give us the vision to minister as a family, Harry was no longer content where he was.

> **GOD AND YOU ARE THE ONLY ONES WHO KNOW WHAT YOUR DESTINY IS AND CAN SEE THAT SPECIFIC DESTINY FULFILLED.**

When a vision is born in your spirit you are not content where you are. It is like sitting on a nest of thorns, because you know there is something else beyond what you are doing.

Harry and I have found peace and joy in teaching together and ministering with our children. The reward is in seeing families restored and lives changed.

SET FREE FROM REALITY

Don't let anyone talk you out of the dream you have in your heart or the vision God places in your spirit. If you have a vision for the world, don't let those around you tell you it is impossible or impractical. If you listen to them, you will start looking at reality.

Reality and truth are not the same thing. Think about this illustration. Trainers chain a baby elephant to a stake when it is too small to pull out the stake. As an adult the elephant never attempts to pull the stake out of the ground because he has been trained to believe he can't pull it out. The elephant sees that stake as reality when the truth is that he has the power to yank that stake out of the ground with one tug.

If Harry had allowed someone like Dr. Roberts, a man he respects and admires, to tell him that though he was a wonderful administrator, he wasn't called to preach from the pulpit, Harry's dream would have been shattered. Harry had always been a behind-the-scenes man. That was reality for a season. However, Harry chose to look at the truth of God's vision to lead a family ministry of reconciliation and restoration.

DON'T BE CHAINED TO THE PAST BY REALITY, BECAUSE THE TRUTH WILL SET YOU FREE FROM IT.

Don't be chained to the past by reality, because the truth will set you free from it. If you look at reality, your dream will be lost, just as Danny's dream of being a doctor on the mission field in the Middle East was lost. Julie showed him the reality of how financially attractive a big city medical practice would be for a man with a family. She may have even threatened him with the reality that she would leave him if he pursued his dream of mission work. Danny lost sight of the truth of God's destiny for him in missions as well as the blessings it would have provided. He settled for "the best," as Lot did in choosing the best land in the valley, when he could have had "the rest"—blessings beyond measure—as Abram discovered when he walked in obedience to God's call.

IMPACTING GENERATIONS

The decisions we make affect future generations as well. For example, if Harry and I had not been obedient to God's call and stepped out in faith to establish Salem Family Ministries, how would Gabrielle have been able to fulfill her destiny in the short six years she had with us? Gabrielle ministered in over 250 services in 1998 and over 100 services in 1999 during her illness. She touched the lives of thousands through those services as well as by television, satellite transmissions, video, music tapes, and books. She told everyone she could about her Jesus as she handed out WWJD (What Would Jesus Do?) bracelets. Many adults don't have such an impact in a lifetime of sixty or seventy years.

Oral Roberts said, "Gabrielle was one of the most prayed-for children in the world." He marveled that, although Salem Family Ministries wasn't a large international TV ministry, wherever he went the first thing people asked was, "How is Gabrielle?" We received faxes and letters from people all over the world who were praying for her. We believe that the impact Gabrielle had and is still having on the world is partially what opened the eyes of so many people to see the destiny of Salem Family Ministries.

Our sons, Harry III and Roman, are also coming into their destinies during their youth because Harry and I were obedient to God's voice. Harry III has taught in youth meetings, warning his peers of the dangers of such products as Pokemon, Harry Potter materials, and electronic and Internet games that are seducing his generation into divination and demonic activities. Roman witnesses love and joy to others through his lively music and by sharing from his heart about how to be the best brother and friend to others. They never let an opportunity pass them by to bring someone to Jesus.

STAY AWAY FROM "BOAT PEOPLE"

Our family would not be fulfilling these callings if we had listened to the opinions of others. Don't let what other people say to you stop you from doing what God has told you to do.

Other people may never get in line. Other people may not hear what God wants you to do. Don't listen to the "boat people," those like the disciples who never got out of the boat with Peter.

Don't listen to what Harry calls the "closet prophets," who try to speak "Thus saith the Lord" over you when not a word of it lines up with the Word of God. One such "self-appointed prophet" approached Harry after one of our services and said, "The Lord has told me to tell you that your daughter wants to come back."

In biblical days when a prophetic word didn't manifest, the person was declared a false prophet and was stoned. Harry was probably looking for a stone the day the false prophet spoke to him about Gabrielle. He said, "You think my daughter is in heaven, walking the streets of gold with our Savior when everything she strove to do in this life was to lead people there, and she wants to come back to this place?"

You have to put the negative people who try to distract you from your dream or vision in their place. When God told me to compete in the Miss America pageant for His glory, very few came into agreement with me. They said, "You're from Choctaw County, Mississippi. You've been crippled and scarred. You'll never make it." Four years in a row I lost. Many people said, "I told you God wasn't in this. You're not supposed to be doing it."

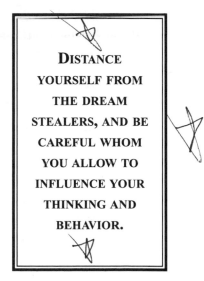

DISTANCE YOURSELF FROM THE DREAM STEALERS, AND BE CAREFUL WHOM YOU ALLOW TO INFLUENCE YOUR THINKING AND BEHAVIOR.

The world tries to rehearse the negative stuff that is against us. They tried it with me. But I knew what the Lord had called me to do, so I just kept going for it. The fifth year, when I won the crown, all these people sang a different tune.

Faith comes by hearing, and you can't walk in faith if all you are hearing is doubt and unbelief. Distance yourself from the dream stealers, and be careful whom you allow to influence your thinking and behavior.

Gabrielle understood this better than most adults do. When someone came to visit and said, "Gabrielle, God is going to heal you." Her immediate response was, "I *am* the healed of the Lord!" If this person persisted in speaking anything but the pure truth of God's Word, she would say, "Daddy, please ask her to leave." She wasn't being rude. She simply knew the importance of surrounding herself with people who walked in faith and spoke the truth.

GOD'S MYSTERIOUS WAYS

You must be careful to discern what God is doing and not jump to conclusions. Here is a good example of how God works in mysterious ways.

We were stranded in the Denver airport for four hours. Before we boarded our plane, I made one last trip to the women's room. A lady followed me and said, "Can I look at your ring?"

I'm thinking, *Why in the world would you want to see my wedding ring?* It was almost scary, but I said, "Sure." The minute I took her hand in mine as she was looking at my ring, the Holy Spirit said, *Talk with her a little bit.* That was an easy request for me to fulfill.

She said, "What do you do?"

I told her that we were in ministry and that our children were with us. She said, "Do you preach in different churches?"

"Yes, right now we are preaching on restoration because our daughter went home to be with Jesus last year."

Immediately, she started crying. Great big tears were running down her face. She had lost her brother and her mother in two separate tragic accidents in the past year and had to settle both of their estates. She hadn't had time to deal with her loss or grieve in the way God means for a Christian to grieve. After sharing with her what we had learned about restoration, we exchanged addresses. We later sent her a tape on trusting God and told her about our book *From Mourning to Morning,* which was about to be released.

As I hurried to board the plane, I realized I had almost missed a divine appointment. Initially when she had approached me I had thought she was a distraction, but I have learned that appointments with destiny are not always what they appear to be. Our conversation was critical to her future destiny, and she was part of my destiny.

Allow yourself to be led by the Holy Spirit to discern the difference between people who are a distraction and those who are part of your destiny. When you know in your heart what God is telling you to do, do it. No matter what you feel or think, you still have to obey God and do what He tells you to do. Don't ever give up. No matter what other people say or do, don't let them offend your heart. Remember, you can't stop people from talking, but you can keep that talking from stopping you!

DESTINY KEYS:

1. Identify the people in your life who are distracting you from your destiny—the dream stealers—and those who are encouraging your God-given dreams and visions— the dream seekers.

2. Determine how you will respond to the dream stealers in the future without being an offense to them. Ask the Lord to give you the right words to speak when the opportunity arises, and practice what you will say.

3. Make a conscious choice to spend quality time with the dream seekers in your life, and make a list of ways to cultivate such relationships.

DISTRACTION 3:
AN OFFENDED
HEART

BY HARRY

D o you know anyone who wears an offense like a badge of honor? For almost thirty years of my life I wore such a badge. I believe the root of my offended heart began when my father died. My childhood was suddenly cut short as I was faced with being the "man" of the house at only ten years old.

My father's last words to me were, "Harry, be strong, never cry or show emotion, never be a sucker for or trust anyone, and confide only in your 'blood' family." I took my responsibility seriously and did exactly as my father said.

Then when people took everything my father had built in the automobile industry away from my mother and appeared to abandon us, I was hurt and wounded. My trust level bottomed out at zero, and I thought *everyone* was against me. From then on I had a chip on my shoulder just waiting to be knocked off. When people approached me, I was quick to rebuff them before they could rebuff me.

Since I also inherited my father's strong work ethic, I was diligent in everything I did and gained a high level of success both in the business world and in ministry. I was striving for perfection in everything I did; but I was doing it *my* way, not God's.

What I didn't realize was that my offended heart was distracting me from the true destiny of God's call on my life. I was working in an internationally known ministry, but I didn't understand I could not win people for Jesus by offending them first. More importantly, by not trusting in anyone but myself, I was unknowingly offending God.

> *The Lord of hosts—regard Him as holy and honor His holy name [by regarding Him as your only hope of safety], and let Him be your fear and let Him be your dread [lest you offend Him by your fear of man and distrust of Him].*
>
> **Isaiah 8:13**

Deep down I feared what man might do to me. I felt I couldn't trust anyone. To be honest, I didn't trust God any more than anyone else. I believed the saying "If it is to be, it is up to me." I had to be in control at all times. Because I did not put my trust in the Lord, He could not heal my offended heart or keep me from stumbling on the way to my destiny.

LET GO OF HEAVY BURDENS

An offended heart will drag you down and cause you to stumble on your way to your destiny. An offended heart is more burdensome than the robe Peter wore as he walked on the water to get to Jesus. As the wind was blowing and the waves were slapping against his legs, his robe must have been soaking up the water like a sponge and pulling him down into the water.

> **AN OFFENDED HEART WILL DRAG YOU DOWN AND CAUSE YOU TO STUMBLE ON YOUR WAY TO YOUR DESTINY.**

You have to understand what a Middle Eastern robe is like. The Lebanese were famous for the rich, colorful dyes they produced and used to dye the royal robes for the royal families in the region. Because of their beautiful work, they had favor with the leaders of many countries.

Being of Lebanese heritage, I was intrigued by these robes on a trip to the Holy Land and brought a complete set home. The robe alone weighs about seven pounds because of the tightly woven fabric from which it is made.

The burden of an offended heart is much heavier than this. Eventually, it will cause you to stumble and fall or sink out of sight.

MEND OLD FENCES

One preacher describes an offense as an old fence that needs mending. The longer the fence lies on the ground untended, the more it deteriorates. The same is true of an offense, which causes division between individuals. The longer an offense is allowed to linger and fester, the more the relationship deteriorates.

> ONE DANGEROUS CHARACTERISTIC OF AN OFFENSE IS THAT, LIKE A VIRUS, IT CAN SPREAD TO OTHERS AND MULTIPLY IN MAGNITUDE.

One dangerous characteristic of an offense is that, like a virus, it can spread to others and multiply in magnitude. More than one church and more than one family have been split apart or destroyed by an insignificant offense that was allowed to fester and then became blown out of proportion.

Satan knows that a house divided cannot stand, and he does everything he can to destroy relationships in families and in the body of believers by using people to hurt us. He also delights in destroying our Christian testimony when we "lose it" in front of others, especially before unbelievers.

We must be vigilant and aware of Satan's lies and tricks to cause us to take up an offense against a family member, a co-worker, a boss, a neighbor, a fellow churchgoer, or even a stranger who cuts us off on a highway, butts in front of us in line, or steals our parking space. When an opportunity for offense occurs, ask yourself, *In the face of eternity does this really matter?* In most cases it is too insignificant to warrant even the aggravation it is causing you.

BEWARE OF PRIDE

One of the major causes of offense is pride, which is rooted in the spirit of haughtiness.

Pride goes before destruction, and a haughty spirit before a fall.

Proverbs 16:18

The spirit of haughtiness manifests itself in criticism, judgment, rudeness, being overly controlling and domineering, and displaying an air of superiority or self-righteousness. This is exactly what Jesus encountered when the Pharisees criticized the disciples for not washing their hands before they ate bread. Here is how Jesus answered them:

> *"Why do you also transgress the commandment of God because of your tradition? For God commanded, saying, 'Honor your father and your mother'; and, 'He who curses father or mother, let him be put to death.' But you say, 'Whoever says to his father or mother, "Whatever profit you might have received from me is a gift to God"—then he need not honor his father or mother.' Thus you have made the commandment of God of no effect by your tradition. Hypocrites! Well did Isaiah prophesy about you, saying: 'These people draw near to Me with their mouth, And honor Me with their lips, But their heart is far from Me. And in vain they worship Me, Teaching as doctrines the commandments of men.'" When He had called the multitude to Himself, He said to them, "Hear and understand:*

> *Not what goes into the mouth defiles a man; but what comes out of the mouth, this defiles a man."*
>
> **Matthew 15:3-11** NKJV

The religious leaders were greatly offended by these words. The tradition of hand washing was more important to them than hearing the words spoken by the Messiah, whom they rejected. Jesus knew that the prideful, critical words spoken by these leaders had defiled their hearts, and they in turn were causing others to fall into their pattern.

Remember one of the seven things God hates, as identified in Proverbs 6:16-19, is a proud look. God opposes the proud. In other words, He won't play on your team if you are puffed up with pride.

Pride was once a stronghold in my life. Employees never wanted to be called into my office. I was quick to offend, so people avoided me like the plague. I resented the isolation, not realizing that it was imposed by my own attitude.

Over the years God has changed my heart, and now many people don't even recognize me as the same man. But don't be misled. There are those who don't want to let you change and try to pull you back to your former self. You can't let people distract you! It hurts, but don't be discouraged or distracted by people and fear of change. In this process, I had to stand on this Scripture many times:

> *"God resists the proud, But gives grace to the humble."*
>
> **James 4:6** NKJV

When Gabrielle was ill and the medical costs were astronomical, one of the hardest things to do was to swallow my pride and accept monetary gifts to help with the expenses. God spoke to people all over the nation to help us, and individuals gave from as little as seven cents to as much as thousands of dollars.

We had to set aside our pride—fear of what man might think of us—and accept the blessings that poured in. As we humbled ourselves, God took over and every bill was paid in full month after month.

DON'T BE ROBBED

Another cause of an offended heart is envy, or jealousy. Jesus faced this opponent when he began teaching in his hometown of Nazareth.

And when the Sabbath had come, He began to teach in the synagogue. And many hearing Him were astonished, saying, "Where did this Man get these things? And what wisdom is this which is given to Him, that such mighty works are performed by His hands! Is this not the carpenter, the Son of Mary, and brother of James, Joses, Judas, and Simon? And are not His sisters here with us?" And they were offended at Him. But Jesus said to them, "A prophet is not without honor except in his own country, among his own relatives, and in his own house." Now He could do no mighty work there, except that He laid His hands on a few sick people and healed them.

Mark 6:2-5 NKJV

How many people in Nazareth were robbed of their destiny because their hearts were offended when they heard Jesus preach? They were defeated by the attitude that said, "Who does He think He is?" In other words, they were defeated by envy.

Another defeating attitude that indicates envy is one that says, "Why are they always getting blessed?"

Don't be condemned if you hear these words from your own mouth ringing from the past in your ears. We are all a work in progress. Just when I thought God had wrung all the pride and envy out of me, He reached down and pressed out some more.

Not long after Gabrielle went home to be with Jesus, I went to lunch with three ministry friends. My heart was still raw and hurting as we adjusted to life here on earth without our precious Gabs. I'll be honest. That day, I was having a pity party as I listened to the other men's conversations revolving around how God was blessing them. One was rejoicing about receiving a large donation, another had just gotten a new airplane, and the third was talking about his new building.

As they talked, I didn't enter into the conversation. Instead, I sat there thinking, *These guys haven't been through half of what we've been through. Why is God blessing them? God, how could You give him my airplane? Our ministry outgrew our office space a long time ago; why haven't You given us a new building?* My thoughts were outlandish in light of how our medical bills had been paid off. Then I actually had the audacity to think, *Why can't we have big supporters like he has?* My heart was offended as I wallowed in self-pity and envy over how God was blessing everyone else. The next morning in church I was still mulling over the previous day's conversation, and I was madder than ever. I couldn't even concentrate on the message or the prophetic word Brother Hagin gave us that morning.

In spite of my bad attitude, God spoke to me as He had done only one other time in my life. He graciously listened to me plead my case of feeling sorry for myself for not having what these other three men had. Then He said, *That's not My fault, Harry. I have placed you at the King's table, but you are still expecting child's portions. The problem is that you are in competition with those men, and you are supposed to be in covenant with them. You must make it right. Go back and apologize to them. When you start rejoicing with them, then I will bless you from the King's table and meet your specific needs, son.*

I swallowed my pride and went back to all three of those men to apologize for my attitude and selfishness. They had no idea what I had been thinking, but they were gracious and quick in their forgiveness. It wasn't easy to do, but I was obedient so that God could move on my behalf to meet my needs.

Since that conversation with God, I try to keep my attitude right and not allow my heart to be offended by envy or jealousy. God is faithfully blessing us.

FORGIVENESS IS THE CURE

If you are harboring an offense in your heart against anyone, now is the time to deal with it. The fastest cure for an offense is forgiveness.

> **THE FASTEST CURE FOR AN OFFENSE IS FORGIVENESS.**

We need to understand that forgiveness is a command, not an option. In Matthew 18:21-22, Peter and Jesus discussed the command to forgive:

Then Peter came up to Him and said, Lord, how many times may my brother sin against me and I forgive him and let it go? [As many as] up to seven times? Jesus answered him, I tell you, not up to seven times, but seventy times seven!

Jesus then told a story to illustrate what this means. We know the story as the parable of the talents. You may be familiar with this story; here is my paraphrase.

A man owed the king a huge debt of 10,000 talents, which is equivalent to about ten million dollars in today's money. (In reality, the man couldn't have even repaid that amount of money if he'd worked until the day he died. It was a debt that could not be paid.) The king wanted the debt paid and threatened to sell the man and his family and everything he owned to pay it. The man begged the king for mercy and asked him for more time to pay the debt. The king showed compassion to the man, forgave (totally cancelled) the debt, and released him to go on his way.

Immediately after leaving the king's chamber this man ran into a man who owed him a debt of 100 denarii, which is about twenty dollars in today's money. The first man grabbed the second man by the throat and demanded that the debt be repaid immediately. When the man begged for mercy and more time to pay the debt, the first man had him thrown in prison.

Other people who witnessed this event went to the king and told him what they had seen. The king ordered the first man, whom he had forgiven, to be brought before him. This is what he said:

You contemptible and wicked attendant! I forgave and cancelled all that [great] debt of yours because you begged me to. And should you not have had pity and mercy on your fellow attendant, as I had pity and mercy on you? And in wrath his master turned him over to the torturers (the jailers), till he should pay all that he owed.

Matthew 18:32-34

Jesus then added this statement, which tells us how God responds to us if we don't forgive those who offend us:

So also My heavenly Father will deal with every one of you if you do not freely forgive your brother from your heart his offenses.

Matthew 18:35

The Father sent His only Son, Jesus Christ, to suffer and die for our sins (debts we cannot pay). When we repent of our sins, God completely cancels them and sets us free because of the blood that was shed on Calvary.

However, if we refuse to forgive others for wrongs they commit against us, we are acting just like the first man in the story and God will turn us over to the jailers. Bitterness will hold us in bondage until we forgive our offenders from our hearts.

BITTERNESS WILL HOLD US IN BONDAGE UNTIL WE FORGIVE OUR OFFENDERS FROM OUR HEARTS.

ONLY BY HIS GRACE

Forgiveness is humanly impossible without God's grace, which we received through the blood that Christ willingly shed on the cross. Sometimes the wrongs people have done to us are so painful that our spirits are wounded. For example, this must certainly be the case for the families of the 169 people who were killed in the Oklahoma City bombing. Nevertheless, though our spirits are wounded, we must forgive our wrongdoers. If we refuse, we will never be free to move beyond the pain.

Most people do not understand that forgiveness is not about feelings or emotions, which are unpredictable and difficult to control. Forgiveness is an act of the will, simply making a decision from your heart to say, "Lord, I am willing to release myself into Your hands so that You can make me willing to forgive this person."

OUR OBEDIENCE IN RELEASING OUR WILLS TO GOD FREES HIM TO HEAL OR CHANGE OUR EMOTIONS UNTIL OUR WILLS LINE UP WITH HIS.

Our obedience in releasing our wills to God frees Him to heal or change our emotions until our wills line up with His. Philippians 2:13 says that God's strength will produce His desires in us:

[Not in your own strength] for it is God Who is all the while effectually at work in you [energizing and creating in you the power and desire], both to will and to work for His good pleasure and satisfaction and delight.

An act of the will requires that we die to self. Only then will we experience true freedom through Christ.

For when a man dies, he is freed (loosed, delivered) from [the power of] sin [among men]. Now if we have died with Christ, we believe that we shall also live with Him.

Romans 6:7,8

Catherine Marshall was a powerful woman of God whose writings include tremendous wisdom and revelation. In her book *Beyond Ourselves,* she wrote this about emotions and forgiveness:

Grudges or resentments are emotions. We cannot get rid of them by saying, "I will no longer feel that way. I shall now love this person who harmed me."

Recognizing the principle of the will, I pray something like this: "Lord, You have plainly told me that all vengeance is Yours, not my business at all. You have said that I must forgive. I am willing to, but I've tried over and over, and the resentments keep surging back. Now I "will" this bitterness over to you. Here—I hold it out to You in my open hand. I promise only that I will not again close my fist and reclaim the resentment. Now I ask You to take it and handle these emotions that I cannot handle."[1]

If you are having difficulty forgiving someone who has offended you, try praying that prayer. I believe it will set you free.

Forgiveness is meant to be given. Once it is kept, it turns into a root of bitterness, which is forgiveness turned inward. Only by releasing your offender through forgiveness will you be truly free.

Once you release the offense to God it no longer belongs to you. Don't go back and try to pick it up again. Lay it down and leave it there. It is in the past, so don't keep rehashing it in your mind. Let God work in the circumstances and in your heart. It may take some time, but He is faithful to complete the work He has begun. You will be amazed how the bitterness and resentment melt away.

LOVE MAKES THE DIFFERENCE

The final step in being set free from an offended heart is to demonstrate love toward those who offend you and to bless them. This may be difficult to imagine, but Jesus gave us His pattern to follow and He also gave us specific instructions.

"Love your enemies, do good to those who hate you, bless those who curse you, and pray for those who spitefully use you. To him who strikes you on the one cheek, offer the other also. And from him who takes away your cloak, do not withhold your tunic either. Give to everyone who asks of you. And from him who takes away your goods do not ask them back. And just as you want men to do to you, you also do to them likewise.

But love your enemies, do good, and lend, hoping for nothing in return; and your reward will be great, and you will be sons of the Most High. For He is kind to the unthankful and evil. Therefore be merciful, just as your Father also is merciful."

Luke 6:27-31,35,36 NKJV

Your destiny is before you. Don't let an offended heart be the stumbling block that keeps you from finding the peace and fulfillment God has for you. If God has put a dream in your heart, press forward with all diligence, with your eyes on Him and your ears open to His voice. Practice forgiving from the heart on a daily basis, and your rewards will be great.

DEVELOP A SPIRIT OF EXCELLENCE

We have talked about how to find freedom from an offended heart, but it is better not to allow others to offend us in the first place. The way to do that is to maintain an excellent spirit. Daniel was said to exhibit an excellent spirit, which represents the nature and character of God seen in the life of Jesus. Let's examine several of the characteristics of an excellent spirit demonstrated by Daniel.

DANIEL WAS SECURE IN HIS IDENTITY AS GOD'S SERVANT

Daniel was so secure in his relationship with God that he was not swayed by anything man did around him or to him. He was not influenced by peer pressure, threats, or even death. He knew the Spirit of God dwelt on him, and he believed and trusted in his God. Therefore, he was not intimidated or offended by anything others said about him or did to him.

DANIEL KEPT HIS HEART PURE

After the people of Judah were taken captive to the land of Babylon, the king of Babylon directed his chief servant to select a group of young men from the noble families of the kingdom of Judah to be groomed for the king's service. This Scripture describes the characteristics of those chosen for such grooming:

Youths without blemish, well-favored in appearance and skillful in all wisdom, discernment, and understanding, apt in learning knowledge, competent to stand and serve in the king's palace—and to teach them the literature and language of the Chaldeans.

Daniel 1:4

Daniel was one of those chosen for the king's service. He learned the ways of his captors, but he never allowed himself to be defiled by their ungodly ways. For example, he refused to eat the rich foods that were unclean according to the laws of the Jewish faith and unhealthy to the body.

Neither was he swayed by riches and gifts offered to him. When King Belshazzar offered him royal robes, gold, and leadership as the third ruler of the kingdom, this was Daniel's reply:

Let your gifts be for yourself and give your rewards to another. However, I will read the writing to the king and make known to him the interpretation.

Daniel 5:17

Do you, like Daniel, keep your heart pure despite the enticements of the world? Or do you find yourself caught up in watching the wrong kinds of movies or following the crowd into sinful activities? Do you keep your body healthy and strong, or are you a fast-food junkie? Do you value the wealth of being a child of God, or are you consumed with "keeping up with the Joneses" and material possessions?

Jesus spoke of how we are to live in the world but not be *of* it. It is time to decide whether your friendship lies with the world or with God. The consequences of this choice are serious.

Do you not know that friendship with the world is enmity with God? Whoever therefore wants to be a friend of the world makes himself an enemy of God.

James 4:4 NKJV

DANIEL RESPECTED AUTHORITY

Daniel willingly placed himself under God's authority, respected the authority under which God placed him on the earth, and did not rebel against the captors of his people. Because he respected authority, Daniel became a man of authority and had many opportunities to demonstrate God's love and to speak the truth of His Word to the heathen kings. Several of these powerful kings bowed their knees to Daniel's God and commanded their people to worship Him.

The kings under whom Daniel served recognized his excellent spirit, and this brought him favor in their eyes. King Belshazzar's mother remembered Daniel and spoke these words to her son when a dream needed to be interpreted:

Because an excellent spirit, knowledge, and understanding to interpret dreams, clarify riddles, and solve knotty problems were found in this same Daniel, whom the king named Belteshazzar. Now let Daniel be called, and he will show the interpretation.

Daniel 5:12

King Darius recognized Daniel's excellent spirit.

Then this Daniel was distinguished above the presidents
and the satraps because an excellent spirit was in him, and
the king thought to set him over the whole realm.

Daniel 6:3

An excellent spirit submits to authority regardless of whether you agree with everything that person believes or does. Daniel didn't agree with the way these ungodly kings ruled, but he always spoke to them with respect because he knew God had placed him under their authority for a season. He submitted to God's choice and found favor.

In our culture, people seem to be generally unfamiliar with the idea of submission. Our society seems to thrive on rebellion, which is often the cause of offense.

To have authority, you must be under authority. Carefully examine how you most often respond to those in authority over you at home, at school, in the workplace, and in the government. If you are having trouble with rebellion against your authority, perhaps it is because you are not submitted to authority at work or to those in the government.

DANIEL HUMBLED HIMSELF AND GAVE GOD ALL THE GLORY

Daniel was a man of great humility. He studied the Word and had an intimate relationship with his Lord. Because of this, Daniel received wisdom and revelation knowledge from the Lord and was able to interpret dreams for the kings and speak with great wisdom.

Though he had gained great favor, Daniel never took credit for anything he did. He was careful to give God all of the glory and praised His name, as this Scripture indicates:

Daniel answered, Blessed be the name of God forever and ever! For wisdom and might are His! He changes the times and the seasons; He removes kings and sets up kings. He gives wisdom to the wise and knowledge to those who have understanding! He reveals the deep and secret things; He knows what is in the darkness, and the light dwells with Him! I thank You and praise You, O God of my fathers, Who has given me wisdom and might and has made known to me now what we desired of You, for You have made known to us the solution to the king's problem.

Daniel 2:20-23

When we keep ourselves humble and seek God's face, as Daniel did, the Lord will use us mightily. An excellent spirit is bathed in humility and thankfulness to God.

DANIEL WAS COMPASSIONATE

Daniel knew that the king's wise men, astrologers, magicians, and enchanters were not getting their power from God, but he didn't judge them. He showed compassion and godly love toward them and saved them from death.

Therefore Daniel went to Arioch, whom the king had appointed to destroy the wise men of Babylon; he went and said thus to him: Do not destroy the wise men of Babylon! Bring me in before the king, and I will show the king the interpretation.

Daniel 2:24

Daniel gave the king God's interpretation and told him that God was the One who had given him the wisdom.

Though Daniel was highly favored in the kingdom, men who were jealous of him tried to have him killed. These men convinced the king to place Daniel in a den with man-eating lions, but he never spoke a word against them.

By his example, we can see an excellent spirit requires unconditional love and compassion regardless of whether it is deserved. Here is what Jesus told us to do:

> *"But I say to you, love your enemies, bless those who curse you, do good to those who hate you, and pray for those who spitefully use you and persecute you, that you may be sons of your Father in heaven; for He makes His sun rise on the evil and on the good, and sends rain on the just and on the unjust."*
>
> **Matthew 5:44,45** NKJV

What steps will you take to put this command into action in your own life?

DANIEL PRAYED

Daniel knew the power of prayer. When King Nebuchadnezzar was seeking an interpretation of a dream, Daniel went to his three friends and they prayed for revelation from God to unravel the secret of that dream. God heard and answered by giving Daniel the interpretation that very night.

Daniel had daily communion with the Lord and prayed three times each day. Even his enemies knew this was his practice.

They tricked the king into issuing a royal statute that for thirty days no one could pray to any god or man except the king. Anyone who disobeyed would be thrown into the lions' den.

Daniel revered God more than man, and his commitment to prayer was unstoppable. Daniel continued his daily prayer in the sight of God and man. He was thrown into the lions' den, but God shut up the mouths of the lions. Daniel was delivered unharmed "because he believed in (relied on, adhered to, and trusted in) his God" (Dan. 6:23).

As we can see from Daniel's life, an excellent spirit requires prayer and a daily time of fellowship and communion with God. This is how we guard our hearts.

> *Keep and guard your heart with all vigilance and above all that you guard, for out of it flow the springs of life.*
>
> **Proverbs 4:23**

An excellent spirit guards against the offenses man and Satan try to bring against it. When we walk in such excellence, gentleness and calmness will put a stop to offense. When the peace of God flows through our hearts, offenses won't have the opportunity to settle there or distract us from our destiny.

DESTINY KEYS:

1. Examine your heart and determine if you are harboring any offenses.

2. Forgive anyone who has offended you.

3. Personalize these Scriptures and read them out loud every day until you believe them in your heart:

And because [I am a *son/daughter*], **God has sent forth the Spirit of His Son into** [my] **heart, crying out, "Abba, Father!" Therefore** [I am] **no longer a slave but a** [son/daughter], **and if a** [son/daughter], **then an heir of God through Christ.**

Galatians 4:6,7 NKJV

Blessed be the God and Father of [my] **Lord Jesus Christ, who has blessed** [me] **with every spiritual blessing in the heavenly places in Christ, just as He chose** [me] **in Him before the foundation of the world, that** [I] **should be holy and without blame before Him in love, having predestined** [me] **to adoption as** [a *son/daughter*] **by Jesus Christ to Himself, according to the good pleasure of His will, to the praise of the glory of His grace, by which He made** [me] **accepted in the Beloved.**

Ephesians 1:3-6 NKJV

DISTRACTION 4: DOUBLE-MINDEDNESS

BY CHERYL

A re you one of those people who never finish one project before you are already involved in several others and then never complete any of them? Do you find it difficult to make a decision and then stick with it? Do you feel as if confusion is your middle name because you waver back and forth on what your purpose in life is? If you answered yes to any of these questions, double-mindedness may be distracting you from God's chosen destiny by breaking your focus.

When we launched out into our family ministry, Harry resigned from his positions with the Roberts' ministries and with Oral Roberts University. I stopped accepting any ministry engagements that didn't include the entire family, and we focused on establishing Salem Family Ministries. It was difficult for some people to accept the changes we made, but we held fast to our vision. We stayed on the road and were only home for twenty days that first year. As a family we were committed to do what God had called us to do. We had to put all other distractions aside and concentrate on this single purpose: coming to Jesus and bringing as many with us as we could.

> **DOUBLE-MINDEDNESS IS NOTHING MORE THAN THE DEVIL'S PLOY TO KEEP US IN A STATE OF CONFUSION AND INDECISION.**

Double-mindedness is nothing more than the devil's ploy to keep us in a state of confusion and indecision.

[For being as he is] a man of two minds (hesitating, dubious, irresolute), [he is] unstable and unreliable and uncertain about everything [he thinks, feels, decides].

James 1:8

DO ONE THING WELL

Children often have many dreams about what they want to do when they grow up. One minute a little boy wants to be a firefighter, and the next he wants to be a race car driver. Harry's father once said to him, "Son, what do you want to do in life?"

"Daddy, I dream of being a pilot, and sometimes I dream of being a baseball player."

"Wait. Wait. Wait. Focus on one thing, and do it extremely well. When you figure out what you do well, you will know what you are called to do. When you do one thing well, all of your dreams will follow right behind you."

You may be saying to yourself, *But there are so many things in life I want to do. I want to get married. I want to have a family. I want to have a successful career.*

Those desires are wonderful, but what is your single purpose? As a family, we have found that when we make coming to Jesus our single, bottom-line, end-of-the-road destiny, everything else God has for us is between us and our destiny.

It is God's good pleasure to give you the desires of your heart, and He knows exactly what you need to accomplish your dreams. The key is to focus on Him, as Matthew 6:33 says:

> **But seek (aim at and strive after) first of all His kingdom and His righteousness (His way of doing and being right), and then all these things taken together will be given you besides.**

What this means is that when you focus on Jesus and His way of doing things, everything God wants you to do will be between you and Him. For example, on my way to Jesus, I became Miss America. As you seek Him in all that you do, you will trip over the right spouse, the right job, the right profession, prosperity, and blessings. You won't miss any of it, because you will run right into it on your way to Jesus. Everything you need is between you and your destiny, because there is *always* provision in the vision.

> **EVERYTHING YOU NEED IS BETWEEN YOU AND YOUR DESTINY, BECAUSE THERE IS *ALWAYS* PROVISION IN THE VISION.**

Why do we allow ourselves to fret and worry about what we should do with our lives and waver back and forth about where we are going or whether we will have what we need to get there? Satan uses such plaguing questions to confuse our purpose and to cause double-mindedness, which is nothing more than doubt and unbelief. If we want to overcome doubt, we must settle in our hearts that God is not a liar and His Word does not fail.

SERVE ONE MASTER

Now is the time to choose whom you will serve. You cannot serve Satan by buying into his lies *and* serve God. Jesus made this very clear in the early days of His ministry when He shared the Sermon on the Mount with His disciples. This is what He said:

> *No one can serve two masters; for either he will hate the one and love the other, or he will stand by and be devoted to one and despise and be against the other. You cannot serve God and mammon (deceitful riches, money, possessions, or whatever is trusted in).*

> **Matthew 6:24**

In this same sermon Jesus clearly pointed out the fruitlessness of worry and unbelief in God's ability to make provision for all of our needs when we serve Him.

Therefore I tell you, stop being perpetually uneasy (anxious and worried) about your life, what you shall eat or what you shall drink; or about your body, what you shall put on. Is no life greater [in quality] than food, and the body [far above and more excellent] than clothing? Look at the birds of the air; they neither sow nor reap nor gather into barns, and yet your heavenly Father keeps feeding them. Are you not worth much more than they? And who of you by worrying and being anxious can add one unit of measure (cubit) to his stature or to the span of his life? And why should you be anxious about clothes? Consider the lilies of the field and learn thoroughly how they grow; they neither toil nor spin. Yet I tell you, even Solomon in all his magnificence (excellence, dignity, and grace) was not arrayed like one of these. But if God so clothes the grass of the field, which today is alive and green and tomorrow is tossed into the furnace, will He not much more surely clothe you, O you of little faith?

Matthew 6:25-30

The last five words of this passage say it all. Combating double-mindedness is a matter of faith. You can't be a doubter and be a person of faith at the same time. The two states of mind don't mix, as we can see in this Scripture passage:

But let endurance and steadfastness and patience have full play and do a thorough work, so that you may be [people] perfectly and fully developed [with no defects], lacking in nothing. If any of you is deficient in wisdom, let him ask of the giving God [Who gives] to everyone liberally and ungrudgingly, without reproaching or faultfinding, and it will be given him. Only it must be in faith that he asks with no wavering (no hesitating, no doubting). For the one who wavers (hesitates, doubts) is like the billowing surge out at

sea that is blown hither and thither and tossed by the wind.
For truly, let not such a person imagine that he will receive
anything [he asks for] from the Lord.

James 1:4-7

What we see here is that being double-minded, wavering,
and hesitating distracts us from our destiny and hinders the
answers to our prayers. God gives us what we need "liberally
and ungrudgingly" when we ask in faith. However, when we are
being tossed back and forth by every wind of doctrine and by
doubt and unbelief, He can't answer our prayers because we are
too unstable and confused in our minds about what we think,
feel, and believe.

When Gabrielle was so sick, we could not stand in faith
believing for her healing and restoration one minute and then
cry and moan about how bad things were the next. We had to
stand strong in our faith in God's Word every single day, regardless of the circumstances we were seeing in the natural. We kept
speaking His Word over her and the circumstances no matter
what happened.

Our destiny was to get Gabrielle to Jesus. Now, for us she
went a little bit ahead of time. Make no mistake, we did not
want her to go at six years of age, but ultimately we wanted her
to go to heaven and be with Jesus.

Some people have asked us, "Well, if you had faith, why
did she die?" We serve a sovereign God, and He *did* answer our
prayers. When she got to Jesus, Gabrielle was healed and
completely restored. God just didn't do it the way we would
have chosen.

The battle of faith versus doubt and unbelief is in the mind. We talked about this battlefield in chapter 2, but we will take it a bit further as we explore the difference between a thought life that is crucified compared to one that is not crucified.

DEVELOP A CRUCIFIED THOUGHT LIFE

Ask yourself this question: "How much of me am I willing to sacrifice to be all of Jesus?"

God continually reminds us that there is no "I" in Jesus. There is only Jesus in us and "us" in Jesus. God established the Holy Trinity as God

THE BATTLE OF FAITH VERSUS DOUBT AND UNBELIEF IS IN THE MIND.

the Father, God the Son, and God the Holy Spirit. Man, however, has created a human trinity of "Me, Myself, and I." To be completely sold out to Jesus, we must crucify our thought lives and sacrifice the "Me, Myself, and I" of our humanness.

A rich young ruler came to Jesus and asked what he had to do to be assured of eternal life. Jesus reminded him of the Ten Commandments, and the young man responded that he had kept all of these commandments since his childhood. Jesus recognized what was missing in this young ruler's life and said:

> *"You still lack one thing. Sell all that you have and distribute to the poor, and you will have treasure in heaven; and come, follow Me." But when he heard this, he became very sorrowful, for he was very rich.*

> *And when Jesus saw that he became very sorrowful, He said, "How hard it is for those who have riches to enter the kingdom of God! For it is easier for a camel to go through the eye of a needle than for a rich man to enter the kingdom of God." And those who heard it said, "Who then can be saved?" But He said, "The things which are impossible with men are possible with God."*
>
> **Luke 18:22-27** NKJV

Jesus saw that the young ruler had too much of "Me, Myself, and I" inside of him and that the riches of this world had made him double-minded. The ruler thought his good works and obedience to the Law would assure him of eternal life. He put his value in earthly riches instead of putting his faith in a God for whom nothing is impossible. He wasn't willing to crucify all of himself to be all of Jesus.

Jesus was crucified on Golgotha, which means "the place of the skull." God was using this as a symbol for us. To be completely crucified with Christ, we must be crucified in "the place of the skull"—our Golgotha, our mind, our thought lives. God knows all of our victories and defeats take place in our minds. All battles must first be won in the mind before they can be manifested in the flesh, or the natural realm.

Many people have Jesus living in their hearts but still have thought lives that are not crucified. Here is what God wants us to recognize. When there is no longer any way for us to figure it out or to find our own way out, only then can God move in and go to work on us and for us! That is why we must surrender our thought lives to Him.

We are not wrestling with the flesh. We are wrestling with demonic forces in the supernatural realm that come against us. In our book *An Angel's Touch* we explain that when you see in the spiritual realm, where the angels dwell, you also see the demons because that is where they abide. The two forces are at war, and when we totally surrender to God, we give reign and power to the angelic forces that God sends to work for us. Ephesians 6:12 says:

> *For we are not wrestling with flesh and blood [contending only with physical opponents], but against the despotisms, against the powers, against [the master spirits who are] the world rulers of this present darkness, against the spirit forces of wickedness in the heavenly (supernatural) sphere.*

As this spiritual battle rages, how, exactly, do we maintain *right* thoughts?

> *The thoughts and purposes of the [consistently} righteous are honest and reliable, but the counsels and designs of the wicked are treacherous.*
>
> **Proverbs 12:5**

To have a good thought life, you must be righteous. If you have righteousness in you, you have *right* thoughts. It is just that simple.

Next, how do we get our thoughts in line with God in order to be walking in righteousness? The answer is in the Word.

> *Roll your works upon the Lord [commit and trust them wholly to Him; He will cause your thoughts to become agreeable to His will, and] so shall your plans be established and succeed.*
>
> **Proverbs 16:3**

SURRENDER DAILY

You first must commit, or submit, your work—what you want to do, your ambitions, everything you want in life—to God. When you do that, you surrender and say, "God, it is yours. I can't do anything else."

You must be positioned and surrendered completely to Him, not just in word but also in deed. God knows the intents of your heart—your motive. If your motive is pure before Him and you give Him all that you have, then He takes your thought life and makes it agreeable to His will.

> **GOD'S WORD IS SIMPLE AND OFTEN HARD, BUT IT IS NEVER IMPOSSIBLE.**

Isn't that wonderful? God's Word is simple and often hard, but it is never impossible. A good thought life comes from daily commitment and surrender to God.

WHAT DO YOU THINK OF YOU?

One important area of our thought lives that we need to examine is self-image. It is not what other people think of you that makes a difference in the outcome of your life; it is what you think of you. What you think in your heart defines the outcome of your life, "For as he thinks in his heart, so is he" (Prov. 23:7 NKJV).

All the time I was in junior high and high school, one leg was shorter than the other because of a car accident. Everyone saw me as a cripple. When I wanted to do certain things, others said, "No, you can't do that; you're a cripple." If a teacher asked me to go to the office to get something, another student would say, "Don't ask her to do that. Let me go. She's a cripple."

If I had listened to what people thought of me, I would still be "a cripple." Instead, every time someone said, "Cheryl's a cripple," I spoke up and said, "No, I'm not; I'm a miracle." Then I jumped up and did what they said I couldn't do. It wasn't what other people thought of me but rather what I thought of myself that determined my outcome. Although they saw me as a cripple, in my mind's eye I saw myself as a miracle. These verses were real in my life:

> *So Jesus answered and said to them, "Have faith in God. For assuredly, I say to you, whoever says to this mountain, 'Be removed and be cast into the sea,' and does not doubt in his heart, but believes that those things he says will be done, he will have whatever he says. Therefore I say to you, whatever things you ask when you pray, believe that you receive them, and you will have them.*
>
> **Mark 11:22-24 NKJV**

I *believed* I was a miracle, and there was no double-mind-edness in me. I lined my thinking and speech up with God's will, and that brought my miracle.

If all it took was for God to say it, everyone would receive his or her miracle because God's miracles are for everyone. It is what you speak out of your mouth and believe in your heart that determines the outcome of your life. When what you say lines up with what God says in His Word, your miracle is launched into orbit by a double portion of mountain-moving strength. If you don't have your own tongue in line and don't know God's Word, then you are asking for trouble.

I was saying to the mountain, "I'm a miracle." Was I a miracle? In many ways I was, but to the world's eye I was a cripple. I had a short leg, I limped, and I had scars on my face. But I saw a miracle. I saw someone who was moving and walking.

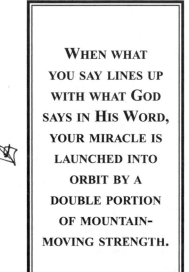

WHEN WHAT YOU SAY LINES UP WITH WHAT GOD SAYS IN HIS WORD, YOUR MIRACLE IS LAUNCHED INTO ORBIT BY A DOUBLE PORTION OF MOUNTAIN-MOVING STRENGTH.

Right after the accident, the doctors had said I might not live through the night. When I lived through the night, they said I would never walk again. I had not listened to what they said; I focused on what God's Word said and believed it in my heart. Seven years later my faith moved the mountain, and I got my miracle in a Kenneth Hagin meeting. My leg grew two inches, and I was no longer a cripple.

Don't listen to what circumstances and situations say to you. If you do, you will be ruled by circumstances and situations and not by God and His Word. Remember this: Losers focus on what they are going *through,* while champions focus on what they are going to.

A good thought life comes from a good self-image. As you think in your heart, so you are. If you want to have a good thought life, think good things about yourself.

When I was competing in the Miss America pageant, people saw me as Cheryl Prewitt, a poor country girl from Choctaw County, Mississippi. I saw myself as Miss America. I saw it in my spirit, in my mind's eye. When I said it with my mouth, people laughed, made fun, and tried to talk me out of it. Yet I never wavered. I knew that if something is important enough, it doesn't matter what other people think, say, or do. What matters is following God.

Did I have what it took to be Miss America? Yes, I did because I had God! That's what it took to win that crown and walk down that runway. Here is what I said: "It took knowing God and knowing that the less of me I had, the more of Him I had. The less of me there was, the better my chances were of winning the title because God is the most beautiful, charismatic, smartest Person there is. He is already everything we've ever wanted to be. As I began to grow up in Him, I learned that when we die to us and become alive in Him, we become the things that we have desired."

MAKE POSITIVE CONFESSIONS

I knew that I had to focus my thoughts on good things rather than on the negative confessions coming out of the mouths of those around me. I understood that what I put into my mind is what comes out of it.

If you are struggling with being double-minded and with a lack of faith, do what this Scripture says:

Whatever things are true, whatever things are noble, whatever things are just, whatever things are pure, whatever

> *things are lovely, whatever things are of good report, if*
> *there is any virtue and if there is anything praiseworthy—*
> *meditate on these things.*

> **Philippians 4:8** NKJV

Meditate, or think, on these things. You may have to think for a while before you can come up with pure, lovely, just, honest, good thoughts, but think until you find them. Don't dwell or meditate on the mess, on what other people say, or on the circumstances. Meditate on a good report, on the truth.

The media is not truthful, so don't meditate on what you read in the newspaper, hear on the evening news, or watch in TV shows or movies. It isn't truthful, just, honest, or pure, and it will mess up your mind. Don't think you can watch a little of it and counteract it. Just let it all go in favor of the truth you will find in God's Word. You might be thinking, *But that's too hard.* The only alternative is to stay in the mess you are in.

If you want to please God and walk in righteousness, you must seek the truth of God's Word and have faith. We cannot please Him without faith, as Hebrews tells us:

> *But without faith it is impossible to please and be satisfactory*
> *to Him. For whoever would come near to God must [neces-*
> *sarily] believe that God exists and that He is the rewarder of*
> *those who earnestly and diligently seek Him [out].*

> **Hebrews 11:6**

How do we get faith?

> *So then faith comes by hearing, and hearing by the word*
> *of God.*

> **Romans 10:17** NKJV

Faith doesn't come by listening to what other people say or by the bombardment of half-truths and twisted thinking that comes from the media. In order to have faith, we must fill our minds with the Word of God and meditate on the goodness and truth of it.

THE PLAN OF FAITH

With the following three verses we see the plan for walking out our faith in Christ (salvation):

But what does it say? The Word (God's message in Christ) is near you, on your lips and in your heart; that is, the Word (the message, the basis and object) of faith which we preach, Because if you acknowledge and confess with your lips that Jesus is Lord and in your heart believe (adhere to, trust in, and rely on the truth) that God raised Him from the dead, you will be saved. For with the heart a person believes (adheres to, trusts in, and relies on Christ) and so is justified (declared righteous, acceptable to God), and with the mouth he confesses (declares openly and speaks out freely his faith) and confirms [his] salvation.

Romans 10:8-10

When we believe, it comes out our lips and is in our hearts. Such is the message of faith that we preach. We acknowledge it with confession.

What we believe is a direct result of our thinking. If we don't think right, we believe wrong. If we believe wrong, we talk wrong. If we talk wrong, we hear wrong. If we hear wrong, we act or do wrong. All this occurs when we feed wrong thinking into ourselves.

The Word of God is given to us to straighten out our thinking. The only cure for double-mindedness is to get into the Word and let God fix your thinking.

The decision to change your thinking is an act of your will, a choice. You must choose to put God first and to think correctly. When you are saved Jesus comes into your heart, but it is up to you to determine how you think and what you believe by transforming your mind through the Word of God.

> *Do not be conformed to this world (this age), [fashioned after and adapted to its external, superficial customs], but be transformed (changed) by the [entire] renewal of your mind [by its new ideals and its new attitude], so that you may prove [for yourselves] what is the good and acceptable and perfect will of God, even the thing which is good and acceptable and perfect [in His sight for you].*

Romans 12:2

How do we renew our minds? We do so by choosing to believe that our minds are worth renewing, that we are special, valuable and can do all things through Christ who strengthens us. We do it by delving into God's Word, by reading good God-filled books, and by listening to anointed teaching tapes over and over again until truth and revelation of His Word fill our innermost beings.

The Word of God won't get into us by osmosis or because we wish it were there. My mother says, "If wishes were horses, we'd all take a ride; wishes are wasteful." Wishes don't get you very far. It takes action to initiate change. If we want to renew our minds, we need to read the same Scriptures repeatedly and get new revelation every time we do so; we need to go to church regularly and hear what God has to say.

Where is the battleground? It is in our minds. Jesus was crucified in "the place of the skull," so we must be crucified in "the place of the skull"—in our minds. Here is an important Scripture on which to meditate in this light:

> *If then you have been raised with Christ [to a new life, thus sharing His resurrection from the dead], aim at and seek the [rich, eternal treasures] that are above, where Christ is, seated at the right hand of God.*

Colossians 3:1

Christ has been crucified. If you are going to be raised with Christ, you must also first be crucified. You have to die first before you can live. You have to be crucified before you can be resurrected.

SATAN PREYS ON DARKNESS IN THE MIND

The territory of a thought life that has not been crucified is Satan's primary target in our lives. Where there is darkness, you will find the devil and his cohorts operating in full force because his dominion is darkness, as Jude 6 reveals:

> *And angels who did not keep (care for, guard, and hold to) their own first place of power but abandoned their proper dwelling place – these*

THE TERRITORY OF A THOUGHT LIFE THAT HAS NOT BEEN CRUCIFIED IS SATAN'S PRIMARY TARGET IN OUR LIVES.

he has reserved in custody in eternal chains (bonds) under
the thick gloom of utter darkness until the judgment and
doom of the great day.

A thought life that is not crucified also abides in spiritual darkness, which gives full reign to evil forces. If you have not crucified your thoughts, there is darkness in your thought life. To defeat Satan in your life, you must first be crucified in "the place of the skull"—in your thought life—and be renewed in your mind and thinking by the Word of God.

There are two kinds of thinking we need to discuss. The first is comfort-zone thinking, or permissible thinking that is not conformed to God's Word. It is what we are used to and allow to go through or to stay in our minds although we know it isn't necessarily godly. We often allow it to be there because it's always been there. We say to ourselves: "It's just the way I am and who I am. It's the way I've always been and the way I've always thought." Fantasies, soap operas, talk shows, newspapers, and movies with bad ratings shape such thinking. Remember this key: If it moves you into fear and out of faith, then it is not what God wants for you.

The second kind of thinking is programmed or reprogrammed thinking, which renews your mind. This type of thinking makes your mind think as God thinks.

Which type of thinking do you make a part of your steady mental diet? How much permissible thinking are you willing to crucify to reprogram your mind to think as God thinks?

Wherever there is willful disobedience to the Word of God, there is spiritual darkness. God cannot tolerate, associate with, or look upon sin. Therefore, in any area (thinking, actions, and so forth) that is not crucified with Christ, there is spiritual darkness and Satan can enter and attack in full force.

I'm not saying Satan can take you over and possess you if you think or do the wrong things, but satanic forces can come against you in areas of your life that have not been crucified. Such areas could be profanity, pornography, addictions of all kinds, pride, anger, bitterness, or anything that is not under the control of the Holy Spirit. Satan dines on what you withhold from God.

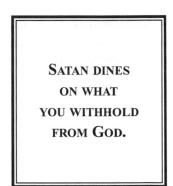

SATAN DINES ON WHAT YOU WITHHOLD FROM GOD.

The light that is in you is the light of Christ, but this Scripture clearly warns that your light can be overshadowed by darkness if you allow it:

> **Be careful, therefore, that the light that is in you is not darkness.**
>
> **Luke 11:35**

It is crucial for you to have light in your heart.

> **The spirit of man [that factor in human personality which proceeds immediately from God] is the lamp of the Lord, searching all his innermost parts.**
>
> **Proverbs 20:27**

God searches our hearts. That is why we need a lot of light—crucified thoughts—in us. Then we can continually be searching out our persons, our reasons, our motives, our desires, and our hopes to make sure they are like God's.

If the light in our thought lives becomes darkness, all of a sudden we will have nothing with which to search and will find ourselves groping around in the darkness where everything looks okay. Darkness in the mind is dangerous because Satan has God-given rights to the domain of darkness. Therefore, any areas that we hide in darkness are areas of our future defeat.

Double-mindedness, which produces doubt and unbelief, resides in the darkness of a thought life that has not been crucified. It must be crucified in order for faith to rise up and lead us into our future destiny.

Christ has called us out of the darkness into His marvelous light to do great and wonderful deeds.

But you are a chosen race, a royal priesthood, a dedicated nation, [God's] own purchased, special people, that you may set forth the wonderful deeds and display the virtues and perfections in Him Who called you out of darkness into His marvelous light.

1 Peter 2:9

God has chosen, purchased, called, and equipped us to live in His marvelous light. Now is the time to crucify our thought lives and turn away from double-mindedness once and for all.

Get into God's Word and find the path that is set before you. Focus on one thing at a time until you do it well. Let faith arise and walk into your destiny.

DESTINY KEYS:

1. Identify areas of your thought life that have not been crucified.

2. Prepare a prioritized plan of action to crucify each of these areas. (Remember, you didn't get this way in a day, and you can't change everything in one day.)

3. Start taking one step at a time today.

4. Focus on doing one thing well, and watch other things fall into place.

DISTRACTION 5:
LACK OF
DIRECTION

BY CHERYL

W ith tear-filled eyes and unspeakable joy in his heart, the conductor raised his baton, the signal for all eyes in the orchestra to focus on him. One dramatic sweep of the baton brought the concert hall to life with the military beat and melodious sound of John Phillip Sousa's "Stars and Stripes Forever" played by none other than the prestigious Boston Pops Orchestra.

What caused tears to well up in this conductor's eyes? This was no ordinary concert, and the conductor was certainly no ordinary musician. It wasn't Arthur Fiedler or John Williams waving the baton with such purpose and skill, totally immersed in directing the performance of a lifetime. It was Brandon, a high school student from Goose Creek, South Carolina, fulfilling an unstoppable dream to personally direct the Boston Pops Orchestra. He wasn't asleep. This dream was really happening because Brandon believed the impossible is possible.

While some boys see themselves playing football in the Super Bowl or winning the World Series in baseball, Brandon saw himself directing an orchestra, more specifically, the Boston Pops Orchestra. Once he caught the vision, he knew his purpose and set his direction to do whatever it took to get there.

Because he believed that it was impossible for a conductor to direct others in an orchestra unless he understands their instruments, Brandon established a goal to learn to play every orchestral instrument. Thus far, he had learned to play twelve instruments.

Next he had researched information about the Boston Pops Orchestra and learned that donors who give $10,000 or more may be given an opportunity to direct the orchestra. Brandon knew he had found a key to open the door to his dream as he set out that summer to earn the money to make such a donation. Working eleven different jobs, including mowing lawns, washing cars, and delivering pizzas, Brandon earned the first $5000 by January of the following year, 2000. He sent the money to the Boston Pops and explained that the remaining $5000 would be forthcoming.

In the late summer of 2000 the Boston Pops Orchestra was scheduled to perform in the Charleston, South Carolina, area. The orchestra invited Brandon to direct one selection at this concert, and they even returned his $5000 to help finance his college education.

He brought down the house with Sousa's popular march and was later interviewed on NBC's *Today Show.* This was not the end of his dream to be a conductor. It was only the beginning.

What was it that kept Brandon moving forward while working eleven different jobs, going to school, and pursuing his music studies? He kept the vision before his eyes, he set clear, attainable goals, he stayed on track, and he didn't allow himself to be distracted regardless of what came his way.

Do you think he was ever tempted to give up? I'm sure he was. Do you think other people tried to tell him he was crazy to think he could direct the Boston Pops? I'm sure they did. Do you think anyone believed he could raise $10,000 all by himself? Not many did. Even his mother said she was skeptical when Brandon told her what he intended to do, because she knew she couldn't help him. She had just lost her job. The reason he wasn't distracted from his dream was that he had a specific direction in which he was headed, and he didn't allow anyone or anything to take him off course.

FOLLOW HIS ROADMAP

Lack of direction is a sure-fire way to be distracted from your destiny and to open the door to confusion regarding your purpose. Everything God has for you to do is between you and Him. If you don't have a good roadmap or clear directions to get to Him, you may find yourself wandering on every back road along the way.

> IF YOU DON'T
> HAVE A GOOD
> ROADMAP OR
> CLEAR DIRECTIONS
> TO GET TO
> HIM, YOU MAY
> FIND YOURSELF
> WANDERING ON
> EVERY BACK ROAD
> ALONG THE WAY.

Harry Salem is a great driver, but he is not the king of direction. He has had lots of practice with the thousands of miles we have put on our motor coach in the last few years, but he doesn't get to our destinations without some help with directions. When he is the driver, I am the navigator.

When Gabrielle went into a medical crisis in Michigan, the doctor said she would have to fly home. That meant I had to fly with her, and Harry had to drive the motor coach back to Tulsa. Our friend, Pastor Ron Clark from Florida, volunteered to ride with Harry. Knowing Harry's sense of direction, I wrote down the specific directions, highlighted the map, and said, "From Kalamazoo to Tulsa is basically four turns onto four interstates." How difficult could that be? I found out later that Pastor Ron just threw it away saying, "Okay. Let's go to Tulsa! Roadtrip!"

After I arrived in Tulsa and got Gabrielle settled down, I called Harry to find out where they were. I said, "You should be coming to Chicago pretty soon."

"Oh, I've already gone through Chicago."

"Very soon, then, you're going to get on 55 South and head toward St. Louis. It's not hard to find your way."

"I'm already on 55."

"Wow, you're making fantastic time."

"We haven't had any trouble. We're on 55 South."

"I'll call you in about three hours. You should be coming to St. Louis. Then you get on I-44 West and you're home. It's just one more turn. You've got it."

I called him about three hours later and said, "Honey, where are you? Are you coming into a big city?"

"Yeah. A big city is right in front of me."

"Well, that's going to be St. Louis. I'll stay on the line and walk you through it until you get onto I-44."

"Here comes the sign now. It says, 'Welcome to Terre Haute.'"

"No, honey. You're on 55 South, right?"

"I'm on 55 South."

"You can't be going into Terre Haute, Indiana, because Terre Haute is not on 55 South. You must have misread the sign."

"No, I'm looking at it right now. It says Terre Haute, Indiana."

"Honey, then you're not on 55."

"I'm on 55. I've been on it for hours."

"Honey, 55 doesn't go to Terre Haute."

"Yes, it does. I'm on 55, and I'm in Terre Haute."

I assured him this was impossible, but he was not moved by what I was saying. He persisted and said, "I'm on 55. In fact, I see a sign coming at me right now, and it says 55...miles per hour!"

If you lose your direction, you will be off track. It was only four turns from Kalamazoo to Tulsa, but one wrong turn took Harry miles out of his way. However, once he turned around and headed in the right direction, he made it home to Tulsa.

> **THE IMPORTANT THING TO UNDERSTAND IS THAT IF WE FIND OURSELVES GOING IN THE WRONG DIRECTION, IT IS NEVER TOO LATE TO TURN AROUND AND GET BACK ON TRACK.**

We can laugh at this story because many of us have experienced something like this. The important thing to understand is that if we find ourselves going in the wrong direction, it is never too late to turn around and get back on track.

LOST IN A MAZE

Losing our direction can be scary unless we stay focused on Jesus, as our friends Joe and Margie Knight learned on a short-term mission trip to southern Spain. Anyone who visits Spain soon discovers that the Spaniards live on a unique time schedule. An afternoon siesta means that everything happening in the evening after a late dinner goes well into the night.

Joe and Margie visited the city of Jerez with their mission group to attend an evening church service. The group had squeezed into three small cars to make the trip to Jerez, which was about two and one-half hours from the small town in which they were staying. They spent the afternoon walking and touring this beautiful old city. The church was located in a very old section of the city, where the streets were narrow and winding. Parking was impossible, and they were forced to park several streets away from the church.

The church service didn't begin until almost nine o'clock and ended just after midnight. Joe decided to go get the car and bring it around to the church entrance. Margie didn't want him to go alone, so she went along after telling one of the other people in their group what they were doing.

Their walk to the car was like a journey into another century. The dark, narrow cobblestone and brick streets were rough to walk on, and the high walls of the buildings blocked any light from the moon or stars. Streetlights were nonexistent. The mission group leader had warned them that this city had a high crime rate because of drug trade and that tourists were often targeted. Auto theft was becoming more frequent. Joe and Margie breathed a sign of relief when they reached the car and found everything in order.

As Joe pulled the car out of the narrow parking space and drove around the corner to turn toward the church, they discovered only one-way streets which were headed away from the church. Each narrow, crooked street took them farther from their intended destination. Before long they lost all sense of direction in the maze of streets and were hopelessly lost.

This was a desperate situation. Joe and Margie didn't speak Spanish, and very few people in the cities of southern Spain spoke English. Margie discovered that she had even forgotten to bring her little pocket Spanish/English dictionary. She began searching the car for the map of the city she had picked up while touring that afternoon, but it was gone. The walkie-talkie the group normally used to communicate between vehicles while driving was not in the car either.

Then they realized neither of them could remember the Spanish name of the church, the street name, or the pastor's name; even if they did find the police station, they wouldn't be able to say where they were trying to go. They didn't see any policemen, and the few people they did see didn't look like anyone they wanted to approach in the middle of the night in a strange city.

By this time it was almost two o'clock in the morning, and they didn't know what to do. One thing was certain. They could do nothing in their own might and were totally dependent on the Lord. Joe drove and Margie prayed in the Spirit, asking for protection and direction back to the church.

At one point they found themselves face-to-face with a chain-link fence on a dead-end street in what appeared to be an industrial/business area, and a car pulled in behind them. This was not good. Joe was able to quickly turn around, and the other car backed up to let them out of what could have been a dangerous trap. It took everything in them not to panic but to stay focused on the Lord, praying and listening for His direction.

Eventually, they found their way to the main street of the city where they had walked earlier in the day. They knew the general direction in which they had walked to the church but could not drive on the same streets because they were too narrow for a car. They kept praying and trying to make their way back to the church.

Suddenly, Margie saw a doorway to an old Catholic church she recognized from their walking tour and knew it was close to where they had parked. Around the next corner they saw several members of their group standing next to the mission group leader's car. Someone had broken into the car and stolen everything in the car and the trunk. One of the church pastor's had come to take them to the police station to report the theft and to report Joe and Margie as missing.

The group had been frantically concerned about Joe and Margie. If it hadn't been for the car break in, they would have left for the police station much earlier, and Joe and Margie would not have found them. They had been driving the streets of the city for more than two and one-half hours.

LESSONS LEARNED

Joe and Margie learned several valuable lessons about direction that night. We can apply these lessons to our own lives as well.

Focus on Jesus

First and foremost, stay focused on Jesus and pray in the Spirit for guidance and protection. Margie said that when she stopped praying and let her mind think about the situation they were in, she could feel fear begin to well up inside. Immediately she went back to praying, and peace returned to her spirit. God was truly in control the whole time.

Have a Plan and Be Prepared for the Unexpected

Second, always have a plan and be prepared for unexpected events and roadblocks. For the remainder of their time in Spain, Joe and Margie were careful to carry with them key names, addresses, and telephone numbers written in Spanish so that someone could guide them if they lost their direction. They made sure the walkie-talkie was charged up and in the car along with the roadmap. They were prepared and were not caught off guard again.

Jesus spoke of the importance of being prepared in the parable about the ten virgins waiting for the bridegroom.

Then the kingdom of heaven shall be likened to ten virgins who took their lamps and went to meet the bridegroom. Five of them were foolish (thoughtless, without fore-thought) and five were wise (sensible, intelligent, and prudent). For when the foolish took their lamps, they did not take any [extra] oil with them; but the wise took flasks of oil along with them [also] with their lamps.

Matthew 25:1-4

The wise virgins had a plan and were prepared to meet the bridegroom whenever he came. The foolish virgins were unprepared and lacked direction. At the last minute they wanted the wise virgins to share their oil, but the wise virgins sent them to buy their own oil. While they were away buying oil, the bridegroom came, and the five foolish virgins missed their opportunity to go into the wedding feast. Here is what the bridegroom (Jesus) said to the foolish virgins when they knocked on the door:

But He replied, I solemnly declare to you, I do not know you
[I am not acquainted with you]. Watch therefore [give strict
attention and be cautious and active], for you know neither
the day nor the hour when the Son of Man will come.

Matthew 25:12,13

We each have a destiny to fulfill in this day and this hour. If we are inattentive of and unprepared for Jesus' coming, we risk being left behind or missing our destiny.

Stay Connected With Believers

Third, don't allow yourself to be separated or isolated from other believers. A lion never attacks an animal in a herd. He watches for one animal to tire and fall back from the rest or to wander off alone. Then he attacks. Our enemy hunts the same way, as this Scripture indicates:

Be sober, be vigilant; because your adversary the devil walks
about like a roaring lion, seeking whom he may devour.

1 Peter 5:8 NKJV

The devil tries to separate us from others so we will be more vulnerable to his tactics and schemes. Even though Joe and Margie had been separated from the group physically while they were wandering around the city, they were connected spiritually. They were praying, and so were the other team members. Even so, they were more vigilant from then on not to allow themselves to be separated from the group without a plan of how and where to meet or make contact again.

Let God Direct You

Last, let go and let God direct your path. God knows exactly where you are at all times, and He knows how to direct your footsteps. Joe and Margie were lost in a strange city, but God knew how to guide them back to their group.

Brandon had a dream to conduct the Boston Pops Orchestra, and God knew how to do the impossible for a committed young man. I had a dream to be Miss America, and God directed my footsteps onto that runway in 1980. Harry and I had a vision for a family ministry, and God has been with us and guided us every step of the way.

What is your dream? Are you willing to let go of it and allow God to take you where you need to go? Are you seeking direction from Him, or are you trying to get there your own way? It is time to settle in your heart that God's way is the best way. Place your destiny in His hands, and you won't be disappointed. Psalm 37:3-4 NKJV says:

> **IT IS TIME TO SETTLE IN YOUR HEART THAT GOD'S WAY IS THE BEST WAY.**

Trust in the Lord, and do good; Dwell in the land, and feed on His faithfulness. Delight yourself also in the Lord, And He shall give you the desires of your heart.

PRAY FOR DIRECTION

If you've had difficulty finding direction for your life, the first step you need to take is to pray. Use these prayer requests as a guide.

1. Ask God to reveal to you His specific purpose for your life and His directions on how to get there.

2. Ask Him to reveal to you specific Scriptures on which to stand regarding your destiny.

3. Ask Him to uncover any hindrances to fulfilling your destiny, such as disobedience, unforgiveness, or bitterness.

4. Ask Him to send the right people into your life to help you walk in righteousness and to remove any who might lead you in the wrong direction.

5. Ask Him to open the right doors before you and to close any that are not part of His plan for your life.

6. Ask Him to provide the necessary resources to reach your destiny.

As you make these requests to the Lord, write down anything He reveals to you so you can focus on taking appropriate action to keep you moving in the right direction, one step at a time.

AVOID CONFUSION

Confusion is a byproduct of lacking clear direction to reach your destiny. Satan is the author of confusion and delights in distracting us with it. What would have happened to Peter if he had gotten halfway to Jesus and then allowed his mind to be confused with questions like this one: "Was I really supposed to get out of the boat, or was I supposed to stay in the boat with the other guys?" Would he have turned around and then floundered in the water, being pulled farther and farther away from Jesus and from the boat?

Harry once heard T. L. Osborn talk about people's destiny and confusion at a ministers' conference. T. L. said, "I don't like it when people say, 'I'm called of God to go out and be a missionary to the world,' and then add, 'but I don't know where to go.'"

Harry wondered what he would tell them.

He said, "I go get a globe, set it in front of the person, and spin it. I take the person's finger and put it on the globe and, wherever it stops, I say, 'That's where you go!' There is no confusion in that. If they don't go, they weren't called to go in the first place. They have to draw a line and figure out what they will do."

This approach may be somewhat simplistic, but the point T. L. was making is that we can't say we have heard from God and then wander around in confusion. Whatever God has spoken to your heart to do, pray about it and develop a plan for how to do it. Find your starting place, and move forward from there. God will be faithful to complete the work He has started in you.

GIVE IT YOUR ALL

Here is one word of wisdom about developing a plan to reach your destiny. Stop doing what you are doing, and give your total focus and commitment to what God has called you to do.

The reason this is so important is that you can't do two things well. When we made a decision to form Salem Family Ministries, I wanted to continue to travel and do my ministry for women *and* minister with the family. I thought I could do it all.

In a conversation with God I said, "It will be like a relay race. I'll just be holding the baton, and when we get ready to stop one and start the other I'll just hand the baton right over. It'll be really easy."

God knew me well enough to know that wasn't going to work, and He said, *Listen. You're going to have to stop doing what you're doing for Me to start something new. Behold, I am doing a new thing.* In other words, God was already doing what was necessary to establish Salem Family Ministries even though I couldn't see it or feel it yet.

We can't keep doing the old, comfortable things and expect God to do a new thing. We can't keep the old man and still become the new man. To try to do so is like saying, "I'm going to stay single and get married at the same time." This kind of thinking is the reason that many people get married but never actually become one. You have to be one or the other. It doesn't work. You have to stop being who you were to become who you are together.

> WE CAN'T KEEP DOING THE OLD, COMFORTABLE THINGS AND EXPECT GOD TO DO A NEW THING.

I kept my maiden name for a long time after we were married, simply because everyone knew me as Cheryl Prewitt, a former Miss America. I finally realized I had to stop being who I was, Cheryl Prewitt, in order to truly become who I am now, simply Cheryl Salem—wife, mother, and ministry partner.

When we started our family ministry, Harry and I had to cut our safety net of the past and look to God to be our safety net. It didn't matter what people said we could or couldn't do. We knew we had to do what God had called us to do. We turned off all the cellular telephones and stayed away from outside influences for almost two years because we didn't need any distractions. It wasn't that we didn't stay in contact with family and friends and love them, but we could not battle the telephone calls from friends saying, "Do you think you're going back? They haven't filled your office yet. Do you think you've tried this long enough?"

We did not just stick our toes in the water. We went off the high dive and cut all the ropes to the past. That is what you have to do with God. God is not going to let you test Him. He says, "Prove Me. If I've called you to do it, then prove Me right or prove Me wrong."

God is never wrong, and He never brings confusion or fear. God wants you to focus on one thing and do it well. When you are faithful with a little, He will give you something bigger. Seek direction from Him and follow His instructions, and you won't go wrong, get off track, or be distracted by the enemy.

DESTINY KEYS:

1. Think about an instance when you have been distracted by a lack of direction.

2. Write down what you would do differently the next time to stay on track.

3. Pray this Scripture as a prayer: "For God knows the thoughts and plans He has for *me*, thoughts and plans for welfare and peace and not for evil to give *me* hope in *my* final outcome" (Jer. 29:11).

Chapter

DISTRACTION 6: TIME

BY HARRY

In today's "instant" society the expression "time is on your side" isn't very popular. When we want something, we want it *now!* Just look at the food products on the market—instant coffee, instant mashed potatoes, instant oatmeal, instant breakfast drinks, and, to top it all, prepackaged bowls of cereal with milk and a spoon. Drive-thru fast food and specialty coffee huts are found on practically every corner. Superstores and convenience stores are open twenty-four hours per day to allow instant access to whatever is desired, day or night.

The desire for instant gratification spills over into every area of life. Many people expect to achieve instant career success without paying any dues. Quick and easy access to divorce allows marriages to dissolve without any work through the real issues. Day trading on the stock market has catapulted many into instant riches and then dumped them into instant poverty, wreaking havoc in families' and businesses' finances. A frenzy of lottery ticket sales for a jackpot of $85 million or more proves the expectation Americans have for instant riches.

The effects of this instant gratification mentality has even spread into many Christians' approach to faith. They want to receive instant answers to prayer and immediate access to God's throne room without preparing their hearts to come in a spirit of humility, worship, and gratitude. When they don't get what they want when they want it, they turn away and give up on God. Satan jumps up and down and says, "Score one for our side," when he sees this happen, because he uses this mentality of instant gratification to distract us from our destiny.

CONSIDER GOD'S TIME CLOCK

God's concept of *soon* doesn't mean *now*. It may not mean tomorrow, next week, next year, or even years from now. The reason is that God sees everything in the span of eternity, and we are looking at things from an earthly perspective. To Him a day is as a thousand years, which means His day consists of more than 8,760,000 hours, while our day is only 24 hours. Doesn't that put our miniscule concept of time into perspective?

What we have to settle in our minds and hearts is that God knows a whole lot more about time than we ever will, and His timing is always perfect. He has placed each of us here on this earth for such a time as this. It is exciting to realize that before the foundations of the earth were formed, He knew we would be living to see this new millennium.

God has a plan and a purpose for us to fulfill. Timing is part of His plan. If we submit our wills to His will, we won't miss anything He has for us. It is when we try to do it in our timing that we find ourselves in trouble.

> **GOD KNOWS A WHOLE LOT MORE ABOUT TIME THAN WE EVER WILL, AND HIS TIMING IS ALWAYS PERFECT.**

When a woman is pregnant, there is a perfect time for her baby to be born. A baby born at five months seldom survives because it hasn't developed enough to live outside the womb. In the same manner, your vision cannot survive if you try to give birth to it too soon, because it will not have gone through the time of preparation and development required for every vision. Don't try to cut short your development time or give up too soon.

Sometimes in a pregnancy the baby remains in the womb longer than necessary, and that causes a whole different range of problems. One day longer than necessary is too long for any woman. For nine months she has targeted on her due date, and by the time it comes, she is ready to finish the birthing process. Your vision is for an appointed time, and waiting too long to give it birth can cause it to die or to miss the mark for which it was intended.

THREE STEPS TO SUCCESS

After the Flood, God gave us the promise that as long as the earth remains there will be seedtime and harvest. (Gen. 8:22.) Recently God gave me revelation that seedtime and harvest should really be three words: seed, time, and harvest. When a *seed* is planted in the ground, it takes *time* to germinate and grow, and then comes the *harvest.* Those are three distinct processes.

The Seed

Satan will always try to talk you out of planting your seed. He'll whisper in your ear, *Don't give that money to the church. If you put that twenty dollars in the offering, you won't be able to buy gasoline this week.* He wants to steal your seed before it goes in the ground because he knows once you plant a seed, it's a done deal. He can't dig it up. That is why it is so important for you to just obey God and get your seed in the ground.

The Time

It is in the second step in the process—time—that you are

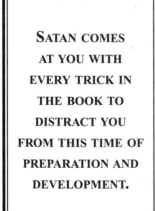

SATAN COMES AT YOU WITH EVERY TRICK IN THE BOOK TO DISTRACT YOU FROM THIS TIME OF PREPARATION AND DEVELOPMENT.

most likely to lose your direction and purpose. Satan comes at you with every trick in the book to distract you from this time of preparation and development. Your heart, thinking, mind, feelings, and flesh all get involved during this time. Take time to prepare because if you don't, then when you are on the front lines of battle you will get hurt.

Don't despise this time. Fill yourself up on the Word of God. Take every opportunity to praise and worship the Lord. Learn how to pray effectively, how to walk in righteousness, how to develop a disciplined lifestyle.

Watching Cheryl give birth to our children I have learned. When a woman is giving birth, the doctor knows exactly when she is to push and when she needs to hold back on pushing. This is known as transitioning, and for the woman it is the most difficult part of the whole birthing process. The doctor guides the baby through the birth canal carefully and gives the mother the right instructions along the way. Likewise, God knows the perfect timing for your vision's birth. You may be pushing and He will say, "Now is the time to hold it." That may be hard to do, but He knows what is best.

It is in the time element or the "prove Me" time that Satan comes at you the strongest. He knows we don't like to wait, and he throws everything at us, trying to get us to quit or to get off track. It was in the

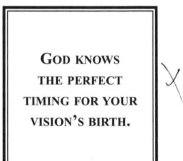

GOD KNOWS THE PERFECT TIMING FOR YOUR VISION'S BIRTH.

time of transition after God spoke to Abraham and Sarah about having a son that they took matters into their own hands and ended up with Ishmael. Their impatience changed the course of history, and we are still seeing the result today with the conflict between the Palestinians and the Jews in Israel. How many times do we create our own Ishmaels because we try to do things our way and in our time?

Sometimes, however, what appears to be a distraction during this preparation time can actually be a signal from God to proceed with caution. God may be trying to protect you from being at the wrong place at the wrong time.

I will illustrate with an example from our traveling experiences. With the hectic traveling pace we maintain, we sometimes encounter delays that are totally out of our control. On one trip, we had been on the road for three weeks and were flying from Atlanta through Tulsa and then on to Spokane, Washington. We had rented a plane to fly from Atlanta to Tulsa, which would have put us in Tulsa at about two in the morning. It was wintertime, and we needed to pick up warmer clothing to go on to Spokane the next day at 5 P.M.

We left Atlanta and got as far as Little Rock when the pilot said, "We have to land because there is ice between Little Rock and Tulsa." We landed, found a hotel, and spent the rest of a short night there. The next morning, we flew on to Tulsa and arrived at about noon. That only left us a few hours to switch out our luggage and be back at the airport to catch our flight to Spokane.

On the next leg of our trip, mechanical problems caused the airline to stand us in Denver. The Denver airport is in the middle of nowhere, and we had to drive twenty miles to find a hotel in which to spend the night. Harry said, "Boy, if we weren't preaching this message 'Distraction from Destiny,' we certainly would be distracted by all of this." We eventually made it to Spokane with time to spare!

We had every opportunity to get angry, frustrated, and upset. But we recognized what was happening and were careful to keep our attitudes right and not react foolishly. What might have happened if we had told the pilot to push on through to Tulsa that icy night? We could have been killed or placed ourselves in a position to miss the whole point of what God was doing.

Sometimes distraction can cause people to do things that are dangerous to themselves and to their destiny. It pays to be cautious and discerning when everything seems to be going from bad to worse in a busy schedule. Take time to ask God what to do, and let patience have its perfect work in you.

DON'T NEGOTIATE WITH THE ENEMY

We must recognize the enemy's tactics and stand our ground, just as Nehemiah did when he was rebuilding the wall in Jerusalem. The enemy wanted to negotiate Nehemiah out of his destiny. Never negotiate with Satan.

NEVER NEGOTIATE WITH SATAN.

And I sent messengers to them, saying, I am doing a great work and cannot come down. Why should the work stop while I leave to come down to you?

Nehemiah 6:3

Four times messengers came to him, and each time he gave the same response. The fifth time a letter was sent with serious accusations against Nehemiah, but again he refused to stop working on the wall. He had a vision and knew his purpose, and he didn't fall for their tactics or threats.

Nehemiah was a man of prayer and courage. The Lord helped him discern what these men were trying to do. He would not allow them to distract him, and the wall was completed as the Lord had spoken. As a result the people of Israel, who had come out of Babylonian captivity and returned to Jerusalem, celebrated the Feast of Tabernacles in Jerusalem with great gladness for the first time since the days of Joshua.

We must learn how to get through our transition time until God's appointed time.

> *For the vision is yet for an appointed time and it hastens to the end [fulfillment]; it will not deceive or disappoint. Though it tarry, wait [earnestly] for it, because it will surely come; it will not be behindhand on its appointed day.*

Habakkuk 2:3

One of the Hebrew root words for wait means "to dance."[1] (Ps. 37:7, Mic. 1:12.) God wants us to learn to praise, to dance, and to glorify Him through the waiting period. If we don't, we will get our eyes off the end result, off our harvest, off our destiny. We cannot have the harvest without a time of waiting.

> **WE CANNOT HAVE THE HARVEST WITHOUT A TIME OF WAITING.**

Often the transition time requires a walk through the refiner's fire. A discussion arose in a ladies' Bible study over the significance of the statement in Malachi 3:3, which says, "He will sit as a refiner and purifier of silver." One lady volunteered to visit a silversmith and to report back to the group more about refining silver.

At the silversmith's shop, she asked, "Sir, do you sit while the work of refining is going on?"

"Oh, yes, ma'am," replied the silversmith. "I must sit with my eye steadily fixed on the furnace, because if the time necessary for refining is exceeded in the slightest degree, the silver will be injured."

It is a comfort to know that even when we are in the refiner's fire, God's loving eye is on us and He knows exactly when to remove us from the fire so we won't be injured or burned.

The silversmith then added, "The only way I know the process of purifying is complete is when I see my own image reflected in the silver."

When Jesus looks at us and sees His own image reflected back, He knows the process of purification and refining is complete in us.

Timing is important to the development of our vision seeds. Every seed has a different germination time. Some grow quickly, and others take much longer. God knew it would be difficult to wait, but here is what He promises for those who don't become weary but wait upon Him:

And let us not grow weary while doing good, for in due season we shall reap if we do not lose heart.

Galatians 6:9 NKJV

But those who wait on the Lord shall renew their strength; they shall mount up with wings like eagles, they shall run and not be weary, they shall walk and not faint.

Isaiah 40:31 NKJV

Peter could not get from the boat to Jesus without time in between. First he had to stand up in the boat in the midst of the storm. Then he stepped out of the boat. You must stand even in the midst of a storm. The wind started to blow stronger, and the rain came down harder. Can't you just hear the guys in the boat saying, "Get back in the boat! Have you lost your mind? It's not really Jesus out there. You're hallucinating. You'll drown before you get there."

Most Christians are, like those disciples, "boat people." They won't step out on the water, and they try to tell you that you shouldn't be out there on the water either.

Peter wasn't swayed by what they said. He said, "That's Jesus out there. I know it's Him, and I'm going to Him. The rest of you can sit in this boat, but I'm getting out and going to Him."

We had boat people trying to distract us from our destiny, saying, "Harry and Cheryl, it's going to ruin your ministry if Gabrielle goes home. It will prove you didn't have enough faith." Peter didn't start to sink until he was almost to Jesus. Then he started to think and feel. Don't let your mind and your emotions stop your destiny.

> **"WHEN GOING DOWN THE ROAD OF LIFE, RIP OFF THE REARVIEW MIRROR."**

Cheryl has a saying that I just love. She says, "When going down the road of life, rip off the rearview mirror." If you don't, you will crash because you can't drive forward looking in the rearview mirror. You have to drive looking at where you are going, toward your destiny.

Several months after Gabrielle's home-going, the Lord spoke to Cheryl and said, *Gabrielle is not in your past, but she is in your future!* That was a life-giving word of encouragement. It helped close the door on grief and mourning and open the door to the brilliance of the morning Son.

The Harvest

Satan may try to steal your seed, and he may try to distract your timing, but your harvest is your harvest. He can't do anything about it. Once a baby is born, you can't put it back. It is here to stay, and so is your harvest—the fulfillment of your destiny and purpose. In fact, your harvest will then become your seed because God has you in a growing cycle all of the time.

Timing is everything! It is vital for fulfilling your destiny. If you stay in God's time frame, provision is there for your vision. It happens as naturally as the birth of a baby.

IF YOU STAY IN GOD'S TIME FRAME, PROVISION IS THERE FOR YOUR VISION.

DESTINY KEYS:

1. Identify at least three time distractions that most often keep you from fulfilling your plans and purpose.

2. List the ways you will eliminate these distractions in the future.

3. Meditate on these Scriptures:

"...For there is a time there for every purpose and for every work."

Ecclesiastes 3:17 NKJV

...And a wise man's heart discerns both time and judgment, because for every matter there is a time and judgment.

Ecclesiastes 8:5,6 NKJV

DISTRACTION 7: THE COMPARISON TRAP

BY CHERYL

Have you ever felt as if God loves everyone else more than He loves you? You look around and everyone else seems to be sailing along without a care in the world while your life is in turmoil. You say to yourself, "They don't have to go through anything. Why is life so much easier for them?"

When you find yourself uttering those words, watch out. You are in danger of falling into the comparison trap, which is a guaranteed way to be distracted from your destiny. We see example after example in the Scriptures of people losing their focus when they fell into this trap.

Cain compared himself with Abel and was so angry when God accepted Abel's offering that he killed his only brother. The older brother of the prodigal son was furious and refused to go into the banquet hall when his father welcomed his wayward younger brother back home with a feast and lavished him with expensive clothing and gifts.

> *Lo, these many years I have been serving you; I never transgressed your commandment at any time; and yet you never gave me a young goat, that I might make merry with my friends. But as soon as this son of yours came, who has devoured your livelihood with harlots, you killed the fatted calf for him.*
>
> **Luke 15:29,30** NKJV

In another biblical scenario, Martha was so upset that her sister Mary was not helping her serve Jesus and their other guests that she complained to Jesus about it.

> *Now it happened as they went that He entered a certain village; and a certain woman named Martha welcomed Him into her house. And she had a sister called Mary, who also sat at Jesus' feet and heard His word. But Martha was distracted with much serving, and she approached Him and said, "Lord, do You not care that my sister has left me to serve alone? Therefore tell her to help me." And Jesus answered and said to her, "Martha, Martha, you are worried and troubled about many things. But one thing is needed, and Mary has chosen that good part, which will not be taken away from her."*
>
> **Luke 10:38-42** NKJV

Martha was distracted by her household duties, while her sister Mary was totally focused on coming to Jesus and listening to His Word. Jesus lovingly rebuked Martha and helped to put her priorities in order.

This trap also distracted Jesus' disciples when they started comparing themselves to each other to determine who was the greatest. It caused dissension within their midst, and Jesus addressed them directly.

> *"You know that those who are considered rulers over the Gentiles lord it over them, and their great ones exercise authority over them. Yet it shall not be so among you; but whoever desires to become great among you shall be your servant. And whoever of you desires to be first shall be slave of all. For even the Son of Man did not come to be served, but to serve, and to give His life a ransom for many."*
>
> **Mark 10:42-45** NKJV

> **IT IS JEALOUSY, WHICH LEADS TO ANGER— A DANGEROUS EMOTION THAT SIDETRACKS MANY FROM REACHING THEIR FULL POTENTIAL.**

What is the root problem we see in all of these examples of the comparison trap? It is jealousy, which leads to anger—a dangerous emotion that sidetracks many from reaching their full potential.

Because of jealousy, Cain committed the first murder and lived as an outcast and a fugitive the remainder of his days. That wasn't God's plan or destiny for Cain.

The apostle Paul warns us about comparing ourselves with others.

Not that we [have the audacity to] venture to class or [even to] compare ourselves with some who exalt and furnish testimonials for themselves! However, when they measure themselves with themselves and compare themselves with one another, they are without understanding and behave unwisely. We, on the other hand, will not boast beyond our legitimate province and proper limit, but will keep within the limits [of our commission which] God has allotted us as our measuring line and which reaches and includes even you.

2 Corinthians 10:12,13

> GOD HAS GIVEN EACH OF US A COMMISSION, A DESTINY TO FULFILL WITHIN HIS PLAN. WHEN WE COMPARE OUR DESTINY WITH OTHERS' WE DISPLAY A LACK OF UNDERSTANDING AND WISDOM.

God has given each of us a commission, a destiny to fulfill within His plan. When we compare our destiny with others' we display a lack of understanding and wisdom. Don't get caught in that trap.

JUST GET THERE!

It doesn't matter how a person gets to his or her destiny. The important thing is to get there. Some people who seem to tiptoe through the tulips may get to their destiny without a scratch or a bruise. Then someone else may take one step into the tulip patch, go down on one knee, and then land on both knees. Before long he may be crawling on his belly in the dirt doing the military crawl. All hell may break out around him, but he keeps moving forward. He may be battered and bruised, but he makes it to his destiny.

Once you get to your destiny, it won't matter whether it was easy or difficult. It won't matter if you were on your belly all the way and could only see His feet. That is how the woman with the issue of blood must have felt:

> *Now a woman, having a flow of blood for twelve years, who had spent all her livelihood on physicians and could not be healed by any, came from behind and touched the border of His garment. And immediately her flow of blood stopped.*

Luke 8:43,44 NKJV

> ONCE YOU GET TO YOUR DESTINY, IT WON'T MATTER WHETHER IT WAS EASY OR DIFFICULT. IT WON'T MATTER IF YOU WERE ON YOUR BELLY ALL THE WAY AND COULD ONLY SEE HIS FEET.

The multitudes crowded in around Jesus. Luke 8:42 says, "The people pressed together around Him [almost suffocating Him]." That means the only way the woman could have touched the hem of His garment was to get down on her hands and knees at His feet. She knew her destiny was in getting to Jesus any way that she could, even if it meant crawling on her hands and knees in the dirt and dust. Her healing was an added reward.

In the face of victory, the pain of getting there quickly fades. The pain of childbirth is quickly forgotten when a mother looks into the eyes of her newborn child. An Olympic athlete standing on the podium with a gold medal around his neck doesn't think about the grueling training and painful injuries suffered in preparing for the final event. Concentrate on standing in front of your Savior and hearing Him say, "Well done. You made it through the fire, and you were not burned. It may have been hard for you, but great is your reward."

When I was diagnosed with colon cancer, after Gabrielle went to heaven, I wanted to go to heaven. God began to deal with me. He reminded me that all my life all I had ever wanted to hear is "Well done." If I had gone to heaven too early, all I would hear is "Well…? Why have you come before you are finished?"

At that point I realized our eternal destiny is always to come to Jesus, but timing is everything.

DESTINY KEYS:

1. Identify situations in the past in which you have allowed the comparison trap to distract you from your destiny.

2. Prepare a plan to avoid falling into that trap in the future.

DISTRACTION 8: FEAR

BY CHERYL

F ear is a powerful force. No one is immune to it. In fact, many of the Bible's greatest characters succumbed to it at one time or another.

For example, the prophet Elijah, who had just called down fire from heaven and killed the prophets of Baal, ran for his life from Jezebel. (1 Kings 19:2,3.)

Gideon didn't feel very courageous hiding in a winepress threshing wheat when the angel of the Lord appeared to him and said, "The Lord is with you, you mighty man of valor!" (Judg. 6:12 NKJV.)

The Israelites wandered in the desert for forty years. A whole generation died without fulfilling their destiny because they were afraid of the giants in the Promised Land and refused to go in and claim what God had given them.

Jonah was so afraid of the people in Nineveh that he ran from God's calling and ended up spending three days in the belly of a whale.

> **KINGDOMS HAVE FALLEN, ARMIES HAVE BEEN DEFEATED, AND DESTINIES HAVE BEEN THWARTED BY FEAR ALONE.**

Kingdoms have fallen, armies have been defeated, and destinies have been thwarted by fear alone. During dark days of World War II, Franklin D. Roosevelt made this profound statement in his inaugural address: "We have nothing to fear but fear itself."[1]

FEAR NOT

God warns against fear hundreds of times in Scripture. Whenever the angel of the Lord appeared to men and women in the Bible, the first words spoken were always "fear not." God wants us to know that He has made provision for His every promise and that He is our place of safety and peace, as He spoke to the prophet Isaiah in this Scripture:

> *For the Lord spoke thus to me with His strong hand [upon me], and warned and instructed me not to walk in the way of this people, saying, Do not call conspiracy [or hard, or holy] all that this people will call conspiracy [or hard, or holy]; neither be in fear of what they fear, nor [make others afraid and] in dread.*
>
> **Isaiah 8:11,12**

In these next verses, He tells us how we are to overcome fear and find His peace:

The Lord of Hosts—regard Him as holy and honor His holy name [by regarding Him as your only hope of safety], and let Him be your fear and let Him be your dread [lest you offend Him by your fear of man and distrust of Him]. And He shall be a sanctuary [a sacred and indestructible asylum to those who reverently fear and trust in Him]; but He shall be a Stone of stumbling and a Rock of offense to both the houses of Israel, a trap and a snare to the inhabitants of Jerusalem.

Isaiah 8:13,14

God was speaking of Jesus in these verses. He is our sanctuary, and He takes our fear upon Himself. God doesn't want us to be afraid of our destiny even in the midst of a storm. All He requires of us is to trust Him.

> GOD DOESN'T WANT US TO BE AFRAID OF OUR DESTINY EVEN IN THE MIDST OF A STORM. ALL HE REQUIRES OF US IS TO TRUST HIM.

JESUS WON'T LET YOU SINK

Earlier we talked about Jesus' walking on the water and how scared the disciples were. When they cried out in fear, He instantly spoke to them, saying, "Take courage! I AM! Stop being afraid" (Matt. 14:27)! Then, verse 31 says that when Peter became fearful of the wind and waves and began to sink, "instantly Jesus reached out His hand and caught and held him, saying to him, O you of little faith, why did you doubt?"

Many overlook the best part of this story. Peter reached his destiny when he made it to Jesus, and then he walked back to the boat with Jesus. It doesn't say Jesus carried Peter back to the boat, so he must have walked beside Him.

> **ISN'T IT COMFORTING TO KNOW THAT WHEN WE ARE IN THE MIDST OF A STORM, JESUS IS RIGHT THERE TO INSTANTLY REACH OUT AND HELP US?**

Then, when they got into the boat, the storm ceased. Isn't it comforting to know that when we are in the midst of a storm, Jesus is right there to instantly reach out and help us? It is even more exciting that once we reach our destiny of coming to Him, we get to walk right alongside Him in miraculous ways.

FEAR IS A SPIRIT

Why, then, are so many Christians easily intimidated and defeated by fear? One reason is that they don't realize that fear is a spirit. How do we know that fear truly is a spirit? Scripture tells us so:

> *For God has not given us a spirit of fear, but of power and of love and of a sound mind.*
>
> **2 Timothy 1:7 NKJV**

Because fear is a spirit, it must be fought with spiritual weapons. The greatest spiritual weapon with which to fight fear is faith. Someone once said, "Faith walks out when fear walks in." I urge you to seriously ponder that statement, because once you open the door to fear, faith fails you. Fear is the opposite of faith, and the two cannot coexist.

Fear attacks our minds and emotions. Peter walked on the water and only began to sink when he started to think and perceive the danger of the wind and the waves. You must stand guard and be filled with the Word of God to immediately be able to respond in faith when you begin to feel or perceive danger.

The foolishness of fear when it is exposed is ridiculous. Imagine Peter as he began to feel his clothes getting heavier and heavier. He let his feelings rule his thoughts, *I'm getting heavier, the wind is getting stronger.* How ridiculous when exposed to the truth! On a clear day, Peter could not have walked on water in the natural.

When you feel fear trying to gain a foothold, you must rise up in the power and the love God has given you and take control of the situation that is trying to start a fire inside you. Praying in the Spirit and speaking the pure Word of God are the most effective weapons you can use against fear.

WE SERVE AN "IF...THEN" GOD

God's Word is filled with promises, each of which is conditional upon some act of obedience on our part. He is an "if...then" God. He says, *"If* you'll do something, *then* I'll do something."

Most people want it to be the other way around. They say, "God, if You'll do this, then I'll do something." But God says, *"If* you, as My child, will do this or do that, *then* I will follow up and do this or do that."

More than twenty times in over fifty Scriptures God said, "If you fear not, I will...." Let's examine twenty of these conditional promises.

"IF YOU FEAR NOT, I WILL..."

(1) *"...Be Your Shield and Reward"*

> *After these things the word of the Lord came to Abram in a vision, saying, "Do not be afraid, Abram. I am your shield, your exceedingly great reward."*
>
> **Genesis 15:1** NKJV

(2) *"...Hear You"*

Do you want God to hear you? If you are in worry or fear, God won't hear you.

> *And God heard the voice of the lad. Then the angel of God called to Hagar out of heaven, and said to her, "What ails you, Hagar? Fear not, for God has heard the voice of the lad where he is.*
>
> **Genesis 21:17** NKJV

(3) *"...Be With You, Multiply You, and Bless You"*

> *And the Lord appeared to him the same night and said, "I am the God of your father Abraham; do not fear, for I am with you. I will bless you and multiply your descendants for My servant Abraham's sake."*
>
> **Genesis 26:24** NKJV

> *"'You will not need to fight in this battle. Position yourselves, stand still and see the salvation of the Lord, who is*

with you, O Judah and Jerusalem!' Do not fear or be dismayed; tomorrow go out against them, for the Lord is with you."

2 Chronicles 20:17 NKJV

(4) *"...Supply Your Finances"*

Would you like your finances to be supplied? If you are afraid, your pocketbook will be empty.

In the following Scripture Joseph's brothers had come to Egypt to buy food for their families and Joseph had ordered that the money they paid be put back in their saddle-bags without their knowledge. God wanted them to know He had supplied their needs, just as He will do for you.

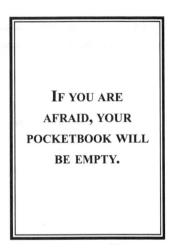

IF YOU ARE AFRAID, YOUR POCKETBOOK WILL BE EMPTY.

"Peace be with you, do not be afraid. Your God and the God of your father has given you treasure in your sacks."

Genesis 43:23 NKJV

(5) *"...Show You My Salvation"*

God can save not only our spirits, but He can also save us out of, or deliver us from, difficult circumstances. If you will fear not, God will show you His salvation, His deliverance.

And Moses said to the people, "Do not be afraid. Stand still, and see the salvation of the Lord, which He will accomplish for you today. For the Egyptians whom you see today, you shall see again no more forever. The Lord will fight for you, and you shall hold your peace."

Exodus 14:13,14 NKJV

(6)   "...Prove You"

You don't have to prove God. You don't have to make His Word true. His Word is always true. If you fear not, He will put a mark of light on you that says, "Here's My living proof." You will be His proof. He will prove you and help you not to sin.

> *And Moses said to the people, "Do not fear; for God has come to test you, and that His fear may be before you, so that you may not sin."*

Exodus 20:20 NKJV

(7)   "...Give You Dreams and Help You Possess Them"

I learned very early that if I wanted my dreams from God to come true, I couldn't be afraid. I have lots of dreams and have accomplished many of them. I have many more yet to be accomplished. God says He will set our dreams before us. If you will not be afraid, He will put dreams right in front of you and help you to possess them.

> *"Look, the Lord your God has set the land before you; go up and possess it, as the Lord God of your fathers has spoken to you; do not fear or be discouraged."*

Deuteronomy 1:21 NKJV

> *So He said, "I am God, the God of your father; do not fear to go down to Egypt, for I will make of you a great nation there."*

Genesis 46:3 NKJV

(8) *"...Deliver Your Enemy and His Land Into Your Hand"*

God will give you the enemy and all of the enemy's possessions, too. The Word says that we can have the wealth of the
sinner. Occasionally, if I see a sinner wearing a beautiful dress,
I say, "Lord, I want that dress at a price I can afford." Then I tell
Him what price, what size, and what color. It is important to be
specific with God.

> *"And the Lord said to me, 'Do not fear him, for I have*
> *delivered him and all his people and his land into your*
> *hand; you shall do to him as you did to Sihon king of the*
> *Amorites, who dwelt at Heshbon.'"*
>
> **Deuteronomy 3:2** NKJV

> *And the Lord said to Joshua, "Do not fear them, for I have*
> *delivered them into your hand; not a man of them shall*
> *stand before you."*
>
> **Joshua 10:8** NKJV

> *Then the Lord said to Moses, "Do not fear him, for I have*
> *delivered him into your hand, with all his people and his*
> *land; and you shall do to him as you did to Sihon king of*
> *the Amorites, who dwelt at Heshbon."*
>
> **Numbers 21:34** NKJV

(9) *"...Fight Your Enemies for You"*

If you will not fear, God will fight your enemies for you.
You don't even have to break a nail or get dirty.

> *And he shall say to them, "Hear, O Israel: Today you are on*
> *the verge of battle with your enemies. Do not let your heart*
> *faint, do not be afraid, and do not tremble or be terrified*

because of them; for the Lord your God is He who goes with you, to fight for you against your enemies, to save you."

Deuteronomy 20:3,4 NKJV

(10) *"...Not Fail You"*

God and His Word never fail.

"Be strong and of good courage, do not fear nor be afraid of them; for the Lord your God, He is the One who goes with you. He will not leave you nor forsake you."

Deuteronomy 31:6 NKJV

And David said to his son Solomon, "Be strong and of good courage, and do it; do not fear nor be dismayed, for the Lord God—my God—will be with you. He will not leave you nor forsake you, until you have finished all the work for the service of the house of the Lord."

1 Chronicles 28:20 NKJV

(11) *"...Not Forsake You"*

Do you fear somebody's leaving you? God says, "I'm not going to leave you. I'm not going to forsake you. I don't care how bad you get; I'm right here with you. I don't care how desperate you are; I'm still here with you. Just don't be afraid."

"And the Lord, He is the One who goes before you. He will be with you, He will not leave you nor forsake you; do not fear nor be dismayed."

Deuteronomy 31:8 NKJV

(12) *"...Help You To Live"*

Have you been walking around like the living dead? If so, it is time for you to become resurrected, not just at church on

Sundays, but in your daily life. God says He will help you to live if you will not walk in fear.

The following psalm has been a mainstay in my life. I declare it over myself daily and have defied death through numerous accidents and even cancer. I prayed it over Gabrielle and know that she did not die but lives in her heavenly home with her best Friend, Jesus.

> *I shall not die, but live, and declare the works of the Lord.*
>
> **Psalm 118:17** NKJV

> *Then the Lord said to him, "Peace be with you; do not fear, you shall not die."*
>
> **Judges 6:23** NKJV

I remind the devil every day that I am living and not dying. I declare the works of the Lord in my life. You just have to remind him. He already knows it, but you have to speak it out of your mouth so it will be released into the heavenly realm. Speak it out and put the devil on notice of what the Word says.

(13) *"...Do All You Ask"*

If you fear not, God will do all you ask. How about that! He said it, so it is true. In the following Scripture, Boaz is speaking to Ruth, but it was God who led her to Boaz and softened Boaz's heart toward her.

> *"And now, my daughter, do not fear. I will do for you all that you request, for all the people of my town know that you are a virtuous woman."*
>
> **Ruth 3:11** NKJV

(14) "...Supply You With Plenty of Angels"

I have seen my guardian angel three times with my own physical eyes. Many times in the spirit realm I see hundreds of angels. Because I have desired it and prayed so long for it, the Lord has opened my spiritual eyes to see angels all the time. If you ever get that close to the spiritual dimension, you'll realize it's not hundreds and hundreds of miles away. No, it's right here, and the angels are with you.

> YOU CAN GO ANYWHERE GOD CALLS YOU TO GO AND NOT BE AFRAID.

You can go anywhere God calls you to go and not be afraid. You may wonder how that is possible, but if you saw what that devil sees, you wouldn't be afraid either. There are more angels on our side than on his side. You don't have to be afraid of anything. You have the right to take authority over every situation, every circumstance.

So he answered, "Do not fear, for those who are with us are more than those who are with them."

2 Kings 6:16 NKJV

(15) "...Be on Your Side"

Did you know that you are a lot bigger in the spirit realm than you are in the natural realm? Years ago I was singing the song "Holy Ground" at a church conference and noticed a woman in the front row who needed prayer. I continued singing and calmly stepped down off the platform, walked toward her, and turned off the microphone so I could pray for her.

There was a man running sound up in the balcony of that church who didn't believe women should be teaching in the pulpit at all.

God has the biggest sense of humor. If you won't get in the way, He'll do what He wants to do.

After the meeting that soundman came to me and said, "Every step you took toward that woman, you got bigger and bigger, not just taller, but with big muscles popping out all over your arms, legs, neck, and face. By the time you reached that woman, you were at least nine or ten feet tall. You were the biggest woman I've ever seen in my life."

He repented of his critical, judgmental heart and rededicated his life to the Lord. His wife, for whom he had been praying for years, was saved that day as well.

He said God showed him this was what the devil sees. The devil sees our spirits, not our weak, puny physical persons. Now, in the spirit, some Christians may look as if they've been in a prison camp awhile. This may explain why when they pray "in the name of Jesus," the devil doesn't tremble and run off. We have the right and the opportunity to fix that by building up our spiritual muscles.

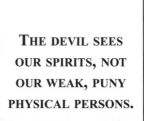

THE DEVIL SEES OUR SPIRITS, NOT OUR WEAK, PUNY PHYSICAL PERSONS.

When the devil looks at me, my spirit doesn't smile. My spirit frowns and looks intimidating. When I flex my spiritual muscles, the demons tremble and the devil runs.

They will run from you as well if you keep yourself built up by praying in the Spirit, reading and speaking His Word, and being led by the Spirit in all that you do. If you fear not, God will be on your side.

> *The right hand of the Lord is exalted; the right hand of the Lord does valiantly. I shall not die, but live, and declare the works of the Lord.*

Psalm 118:16,17 NKJV

(16)   *"...Will Strengthen You and Help You"*

We all want God to strengthen us, but He's not going to do it until we do something. When we first take courage and decide not to be afraid, then strength will follow. It is our choice.

> *"Fear not, for I am with you; be not dismayed, for I am your God. I will strengthen you, yes, I will help you, I will uphold you with My righteous right hand."*

Isaiah 41:10 NKJV

> *"For I, the Lord your God, will hold your right hand, saying to you, 'Fear not, I will help you.'"*

Isaiah 41:13 NKJV

As you begin to speak these Scriptures over yourself and walk in the truth of what the Word says, you may not feel any difference at first. Don't worry; in the beginning, it will just be confession. However, the more you confess it, the more you will believe it. The more you believe it, the more you will act like it. The more you act like it, the more you will become it.

(17)   *"...Will Redeem You and Call You by Name"*

How precious it is to hear the Lord speak your name and know He acknowledges you as His own.

> *But now, thus says the Lord, who created you, O Jacob, and He who formed you, O Israel: "Fear not, for I have redeemed you; I have called you by your name; You are Mine."*

Isaiah 43:1 NKJV

(18)   *"...Pour His Spirit and His Blessing Upon Your Offspring"*

If we will not fear, God will anoint and bless our children and descendents.

> *"Thus says the Lord who made you and formed you from the womb, who will help you: 'Fear not, O Jacob My servant; and you, Jeshurun, whom I have chosen. For I will pour water on him who is thirsty, and floods on the dry ground; I will pour My Spirit on your descendants, and My blessing on your offspring.'"*

Isaiah 44:2,3 NKJV

For the sake of your children alone, you should make the choice not to be afraid.

I'm telling you, the spirit of God is all over our sons, Harry III and Roman, because God has poured His Spirit upon our seed and His blessing is upon our offspring.

Gabrielle's anointing was more powerful than mine because God multiplied my anointing in her. She is our treasure bridging the gap between earth and heaven.

> YOUR CHILDREN DESERVE TO HAVE THE SPIRIT OF GOD POURED ALL OVER THEM AND TO BE BLESSED FROM THEIR HEADS TO THEIR TOES.

Your children deserve to have the Spirit of God poured all over them and to be blessed from their heads to their toes.

(19)   "...Heal You"

Jairus, whose little daughter was deathly ill, was with Jesus when He healed the woman with the issue of blood. Others came and told Jairus his daughter was dead, but Jesus said, "Do not be afraid; only believe, and she will be made well" (Luke 8:50 NKJV). The woman's healing strengthened Jairus's faith, and he believed what Jesus said to him rather than the report from those who said his daughter was dead.

Likewise, when the doctors gave us the evil report that Gabrielle had an inoperable brain tumor, we chose not to accept their report. We heard it but didn't accept it into our spirit.

When I was in a car accident as a child, I had to stand up and say, "I am not going to be afraid to get my healing. I don't care if others don't believe He heals today. I don't care if the whole church comes to tell me I'm supposed to be crippled. I don't care if the pastor and the Sunday school teachers, say to me, 'You've got to accept this fact, honey; you're going to be crippled the rest of your life.'"

You must decide whom you will believe. If Jesus speaks the truth, are you going to believe Him or the people around you? I had to stand in the face of everybody I knew and loved and say, "I don't care what you say; God says He will heal me. I don't care what you believe; I believe God has healed me. I don't care what you think; I *am* healed!" I'll tell you what, *after* you're healed, they will all agree with you.

Forget about the "what ifs." Is God going to heal you or not? God healed me. He healed me once. He healed me twice. He has healed me many times since. And He will heal me till He is finished with me. The Word didn't say I have to get sick to die. If God wants to take me home I'm ready anytime, but I'm not going to get sick in order to go. You don't have to either.

(20)   *"...Make You Perfect in Love"*

God has promised you so many things that you can possess if you just grab hold of them and run. I think the devil had figured out by the time I was in college that he couldn't get me or defeat me. As a freshman in a secular university in Mississippi, I shared my testimony of the Gospel with everyone who would listen. Word spread quickly about whom I represented, and when girls in the dormitory were in trouble they came running to me. I shared with them how God could straighten them out. My Christian roommate and I turned that university upside down for God.

Undoubtedly, we made the devil really mad; we had invaded his territory. Every night my roommate and I read the Word together and prayed in the Spirit. We prayed for our families, our friends, and our dorm-mates. We prayed for God's protection over everyone and everything before we went to sleep.

One night after praying, we lay down in our two metal beds, but neither one of us went to sleep right away. The room was dark, and within a matter of minutes I knew there was a spirit in that room. It was a spirit of fear. The end of my bed came up off the floor three or four feet; it was in such an inclined position that I had to hold on to the sides of the bed to keep from falling out. Fear tried its best to get a grip on me. This was not something I was imagining; my bed was off the floor. My roommate was in her bed, and the door was locked, so who was holding my bed up off the floor?

At this point I hadn't opened my eyes. I guess I thought if I just kept them closed, maybe he would go away. Finally, I opened my eyes and in the ceiling of the room was the blackest black form I've ever seen. It was so much darker than darkness that it made the rest of the room look like a light was on. It covered almost the entire ceiling. I knew in my heart that a spirit had come to kill me. I began to rebuke it, and my roommate, who was really in tune with the Spirit, began to rebuke it, saying, "In Jesus' name, you will not have our lives. You will not take us; you cannot stop us from doing what God has called us to do."

I won't lie to you. When we first started rebuking it, I was speaking and trembling at the same time because I had never faced this before. (There may be times and situations in your life that you tremble, but make sure that while you're trembling you're speaking the right words with authority in Jesus' name.) My flesh may have been trembling, but my spirit was rising up. The more we spoke the Word of God, the stronger we got.

After what seemed to be several minutes, the end of my bed just dropped down on the floor—clang, clang. I jumped off of my bed and got on my roommate's bed, and we grabbed our Bibles, which were always on the floor beside us. We began to read the Word aloud because we were too scared to do anything else. The more we read, the stronger we became and the less scared we felt. We read and prayed all night long.

That night I discovered that the devil could never defeat me in any way, even in his own form. To this day I've never been afraid of him. I've never trembled again in his face, and I will never tremble again. Why is this so? It is because I know who I am in Christ and within me is God's boldness, which has been perfected in love.

> THERE MAY BE TIMES AND SITUATIONS IN YOUR LIFE THAT YOU TREMBLE, BUT MAKE SURE THAT WHILE YOU'RE TREMBLING YOU'RE SPEAKING THE RIGHT WORDS WITH AUTHORITY IN JESUS' NAME.

Love has been perfected among us in this: that we may have boldness in the day of judgment; because as He is, so are we in this world. There is no fear in love; but perfect love casts out fear, because fear involves torment. But he who fears has not been made perfect in love.

1 John 4:17,18 NKJV

Even if war comes against me I will not fear, because the Word says:

Though an army may encamp against me, my heart shall not fear; though war may rise against me, in this I will be confident.

Psalm 27:3 NKJV

If people come against me I will not fear, because the Word says:

For I hear the slander of many; fear is on every side; while they take counsel together against me, they scheme to take away my life. But as for me, I trust in You, O Lord; I say, "You are my God."

Psalm 31:13,14 NKJV

If the whole world is destroyed I will not fear, because God is on my side.

Therefore we will not fear, even though the earth be removed, and though the mountains be carried into the midst of the sea; though its waters roar and be troubled, though the mountains shake with its swelling. There is a river whose streams shall make glad the city of God, the holy place of the tabernacle of the Most High. God is in the midst of her, she shall not be moved; God shall help her, just at the break of dawn. The nations raged, the kingdoms were moved; He uttered His voice, the earth melted. The Lord of hosts is with us; the God of Jacob is our refuge.

Psalm 46:2-7 NKJV

If you have the same Jesus living in you as I do, then you don't need to tremble in fear either. God has called you to fulfill a great destiny, and He has provided everything you need to do it. He is right there by your side, walking with you every step of the way.

Fear cannot defeat you unless you allow it to get its claws into you. You have all the weapons you need, so don't let the devil distract you or take you down by consuming you with fear. Stand on God's Word and in the power of His might. It is your right. Take the land that belongs to you, and don't ever back down.

DESTINY KEYS:

> **FEAR CANNOT DEFEAT YOU UNLESS YOU ALLOW IT TO GET ITS CLAWS INTO YOU.**

1. Identify ways in which fear has distracted you in the past.

2. Determine how you will respond to such distractions in the future, and select specific Scriptures to memorize so they will entrench your spirit.

3. Speak this Word over yourself when you are under attack:

   [I am] *of God, little children, and have overcome them, because He who is in* [me] *is greater than he who is in the world.*

   1 John 4:4 NKJV

DISTRACTION-BUSTER FORMULA

BY HARRY

D o you feel overwhelmed by all of the distractions in your life? Do you want to know how to break free from them?

We all have those days when we don't think we can go another step, but the good news is that our God is bigger than any distraction the enemy puts in our paths.

The key is to stop looking at the circumstances and focus your eyes on *the answer*—Jesus—because He makes a way where there seems to be no way.

> **THE GOOD NEWS IS THAT OUR GOD IS BIGGER THAN ANY DISTRACTION THE ENEMY PUTS IN OUR PATHS.**

The prophet Isaiah prophesied that Jesus would make a way for the blind to see, the deaf to hear, the lame to walk, the lepers to be healed. He even proclaimed that Jesus would make streams in the desert and a highway upon which His redeemed would walk in safety and everlasting joy. (Isa. 35:5-10.)

Jesus has done all these things for us, but it is up to us to follow the formula He gave us to walk in such victory.

Oral Roberts has a three-step formula for success. Cheryl and I have seen it work in our lives and in the lives of others around us. It is quite simple. Here are the three steps:

1. Find out the will of God for your life.

2. Confer no more with flesh and blood. In other words, once you hear from God, don't keep looking to man for answers or direction.

3. Get it done at all costs.

FINDING THE WILL OF GOD

Many Christians struggle with step one—finding the will of God—because they make it more difficult than it really is. When we seek His perfect will, everything else falls into place. Cheryl and I minister to people out of our life experiences, and we want to share with you what we have learned about seeking God's will.

If I could have any desire fulfilled for my children, what would it be? I want my children to know the Lord intimately and to serve Him all of their lives. I want them to have a loving family, a comfortable home, transportation, and every physical need met. However, the most important thing I want is for them to be in the perfect will of God. They are my children, and I love them dearly. I want them to be blessed and to prosper in everything they do.

If I feel that way as an earthly father, what do you think the heavenly Father wants for you? He loves us so much more than our human minds can comprehend. He has already demonstrated how much He loves us by sending His Son to die for you and me.

Jesus came to earth to do the will of the Father. He is our Pattern. If we want to find out what His will is for each of our lives, the place to start is to do what Jesus said in this verse:

But seek (aim at and strive after) first of all His kingdom and His righteousness (His way of doing and being right), and then all these things taken together will be given you besides.

Matthew 6:33

When you seek God's way of doing and being right, everything else will come into place and fall into the order God intended. If you don't know what to do with your life, seek God. Don't seek what to do; seek God. He knows what to do and how you are supposed to do it, and He will order your steps.

> **WHEN YOU SEEK GOD'S WAY OF DOING AND BEING RIGHT, EVERYTHING ELSE WILL COME INTO PLACE AND FALL INTO THE ORDER GOD INTENDED.**

OBEDIENCE DISCIPLINE = BLESSINGS

Seeking God is really simple, but it takes obedience and discipline. Those two words are not popular in the independent and rebellious world in which we live. Have you ever tried to worship the Lord in church while your children are fidgeting and making noise right next to you? Even when you are humanly distracted, you can discipline yourself to enter in to worship.

In our book *From Mourning to Morning,* Cheryl shared how battle weary she was after Gabrielle's home-going and how difficult it was to pray or stay in the Word. She found that the longer she stayed out of communion with the Lord, the harder it was to get back into her daily intimacy with Him. She had to discipline herself to get her prayer life and Bible study time back in gear. When she did, her hunger for His presence returned quickly.

Obedience brings blessings in many forms. During the first year of our family ministry, the Lord encouraged us to teach children how to do spiritual warfare. We believe this is God's form of "preventative Word." It works just like preventative medicine. If we can get the Word in the children before we lose them to the world, we won't have to go get them back when they become teenagers or adults.

We feel called to keep this present and next generation for God. The only way to do that is to teach them how to walk in the Word and how to pray in and be led by the Holy Spirit. Even children as young as two and three years old can be taught how to follow God if we put it on their level.

We couldn't figure out how God wanted us to do it, until He showed us a comic book. He said, *You've got to capture their attention through what they see.* Children are visual learners, especially before they become strong readers. We found an artist to design our first comic book with bright, colorful pictures showing demons and angels fighting over the children's thoughts to destroy the peace in a Christian family's home. One young boy who is full of the Holy Spirit starts speaking the Word of God out of his mouth, and when he does God's forces become so strong that the demonic forces are forced to leave.

In obedience, we stepped out in faith to print this first book, *A Fight in the Heavenlies.* Surprisingly enough, we could not find a publisher that wanted to take this project, so we did it ourselves. We didn't know where the funds were going to come from to do the production and printing, but we believed in faith. God provided, and we were able to give away the first 10,000 books to an inner city children's ministry. The second and third books in this supernatural warriors' action series have also been produced. These books have become powerful tools to impart the Spirit of God into children in a fun, exciting way that will make them hungry for more of His Word, more of His power to fight the enemy, and more of Him.

We didn't know how to do it, but God did. When we were obedient, His provision was there to make it happen.

PROTECT YOUR HEART

Several years ago when Cheryl was sick with clinical depression, we had to go back to the Word and start filling her spirit with the Word. Her mind was so consumed, beaten down, and depleted that it couldn't tell her to get well. So her spirit had to be fed.

People were coming up to Cheryl and saying, "I think you're bulimic. I think you're anorexic. I think you're working too hard. I think you've taken your calling too seriously. I think, I think, I think, I think." They were bombarding and manipulating her mind.

Your mind can be manipulated by day-to-day events and circumstances or by what you see. However, your heart can't be manipulated. It has to change. The words these people were speaking did not activate Cheryl's spirit. They weren't witnessing to her spirit. They weren't witnessing to my spirit. If we had listened to these people, we would have bought into what they were saying.

> **YOUR HEART MUST STAND ON WHAT IT KNOWS—THE WORD OF GOD—AND THAT WILL PROTECT YOU THROUGH THE TIMES OF SEARCHING FOR HIS PERFECT WILL.**

If you get in agreement with the thoughts that come into your mind, you will begin manifesting what you're thinking. That is why, when you are trying to discern the will of God, it is so critical to protect what you believe. What you believe, many times, is not what you're being fed, or what you're thinking. You cannot let thoughts get into your heart. Your heart must stand on what it knows— the Word of God—and that will protect you through the times of searching for His perfect will.

KNOW HIS WILL

While Cheryl was under that spirit of depression and believing God for her healing, she had to discipline herself because she didn't feel like worshiping God. She didn't *feel* like praising Jesus or acting like Him, but she disciplined herself to do it anyway. She knew what she believed in her heart, and she disciplined herself to obey what she believed, whether she felt like it or not. If we will discipline our minds, despite how we feel and act, in obedience to God's Word, we will know and obey the will of God.

> IF WE WILL DISCIPLINE OUR MINDS, DESPITE HOW WE FEEL AND ACT, IN OBEDIENCE TO GOD'S WORD, WE WILL KNOW AND OBEY THE WILL OF GOD.

The plans of the mind and orderly thinking belong to man, but from the Lord comes the [wise] answer of the tongue. All the ways of a man are pure in his own eyes, but the Lord weighs the spirits (the thoughts and intents of the heart). Roll your works upon the Lord [commit and trust them wholly to Him; He will cause your thoughts to become agreeable to His will, and] so shall your plans be established and succeed. The Lord has made everything [to accommodate itself and contribute] to its own end and His own purpose— even the wicked [are fitted for their role] for the day of calamity and evil.

Proverbs 16:1-4

It takes action on our part to know the will of God. We have to *do* something to know God's will. This Scripture lays out three actions that we must take to know God's will. First, we must *roll* our work upon the Lord. Second, we must *commit* our work to the Lord. Third, we must *trust* God with our work.

> **IT TAKES ACTION ON OUR PART TO KNOW THE WILL OF GOD. WE HAVE TO *DO* SOMETHING TO KNOW GOD'S WILL.**

Roll It on the Lord

Whatever you are believing God to do for you is what you must roll upon Him. If you are believing for restoration in your marriage, roll it upon the Lord. In other words, quit worrying about it and give it to Him.

Why do we wait until we've exhausted every human way possible before we finally give it to the Lord? Why do we try to do it our way, according to our wills? If we could have solved it, don't you think we already would have?

The Lord won't do anything about our situations until we take our hands off and release them to Him. He won't bypass our wills. Therefore, we have to make a conscious choice to roll our work upon Him.

Commit It to the Lord

Then God says, "Commit it to Me." Why does He say that? He knows that once we give it to Him, if we're not disciplined and truly committed, we will pick it up and take it back. We must not only give it to Him, but then we must commit it to Him.

A wife can't say, "Lord, I'm giving you my husband," and then in the next breath say, "Oh God, I'm so afraid he will leave me." Once she says those words of doubt, she has absolutely nullified and voided step one. She hasn't really rolled it upon the Lord. She was just pretending she did.

If we really roll our work upon the Lord, we discipline our minds not to worry, not to be afraid, not to be anxious. We commit it to Him.

Trust Him With It

How do you know if you have really done step two? When you commit it to the Lord, you must trust Him completely with it. If you don't have a close enough relationship with the Lord to believe that He can take care of it, then you will have a hard time rolling it over on Him and committing it to Him.

Think about it from a natural perspective. If I don't trust you to take care of something I have asked you to do, I will come back and keep checking on you to make sure you're doing it right—my way.

Contrarily, if you truly trust God to take care of your situations and change what needs to be changed, you can let Him take care of it without worrying about it. He will complete the work according to His own purpose. You have to teach, or discipline, yourself to roll your dreams and desires upon the Lord, commit them to Him, and then trust Him to do what is best for you according to His perfect plan and purpose.

PRAY GOD'S PERFECT WILL

Prayer begins when the human mind ceases to understand. When you can no longer figure it out mentally, in your own human understanding, something else takes over: It is

163

what we call our prayer language. That is what comes out of your spirit and takes over your prayer, because your human mind can't figure it out anymore.

> **PRAYER BEGINS WHEN THE HUMAN MIND CEASES TO UNDERSTAND.**

If you feel as if you just have to pray about a situation but don't know what to pray, then pray in tongues—in your heavenly prayer language. When you pray in tongues, you pray God's will into existence. Without knowing what you're praying, the words coming out of your mouth are speaking God's will into the atmosphere for every demon in hell to hear. This is what is called praying in the Spirit, because the Holy Spirit is the One who gives you the words to pray.

If you continue to pray with your mind in doubt and unbelief, then you will manifest what is filling your mind. However, if you'll roll it over to God, commit it to Him, and trust Him with it, you will be taking the first step in knowing the will of God.

We learned in the last chapter that God is an "if...then" God. One of His conditional promises is *"If* you delight yourself in Me, *then* I will give you the desires of your heart." We want God to do it the other way around. We want Him to do something first and prove Himself to us; then, we reason, we will believe and delight in Him.

Many TV shows portray people's relationships with God in such a manner. I was watching a show the other night, and someone who was in a really bad situation said, "God, if You get me out of this, I'll never do this again."

That is the way we treat God, but that's not the way God works. He will respond to what you obediently do for Him. You have to take action first.

That is why we dedicated our children to the Lord. We gave God our children, and now we believe He will give us the plan, the roadmap, for each of their lives so that they will be in God's perfect will. Gabrielle is already there, but for Harry III and Roman we will continue to do what this Scripture says:

> *Train up a child in the way he should go [and in keeping with his individual gift or bent], and when he is old he will not depart from it.*

> **Proverbs 22:6**

Though we may not know exactly what He has called them to do, we are training them up in the way that each one is bent, according to each one's God-given giftings, not according to what Cheryl or I think they should be. If we train them as the Word says, we know they will not depart from God's perfect will for them.

If you want to know God's will for your life, start asking yourself, "What are my gifts? What can I do for God, and what can I be for God?" Start stirring up your God-given gifts.

The Bible says, "A man's gift makes room for him and brings him before great men" (Prov. 18:16). When you worship and praise God, you stir up God's gifts in you, and those gifts will bring you before great men. Keep your gifts—works—stirred up.

DO IT GOD'S WAY

If you roll your works upon the Lord, *if* you commit your works to Him, and if you trust Him with your works, *then* God will cause your thoughts to become agreeable to His will, establish your plan, and cause your plan to succeed.

This is important for you to understand. You are *not* responsible to establish your plan or to make your plan succeed. You *are* responsible to roll your work upon the Lord, to commit your work to Him, and to trust Him to take care of it.

What a load that takes off your shoulders! All the stress and worry of how to do and be all you think you have to be for God is gone. It's not up to you. It's up to Him, and you don't have to worry about His part. He will do it because He is "alert and active, watching over [His] word to perform it" (Jer. 1:12).

Check yourself though. Are you doing your part, so that He can do His part? This is the rule He put into motion: "If you do this, then I will do this." If you don't like it, you can stand over in the corner and pout all day long, or until He comes through the clouds in glory, but God isn't going to change His rule.

Too much of the time we act like children, stomping our feet and saying, "I don't like this rule. I'm not going to play anymore." We're too busy whining about the problem, saying, "You don't know how bad it is. You don't know how long it's bothered me. You don't know how deep I'm in debt...." We are focused on the problem rather than the solution: Jesus.

It is time to stop complaining with our mouths and start seeking Him through our spirits. This will activate our minds to start thinking the way we're supposed to think, and then we'll be in God's will.

> **IT IS TIME TO STOP COMPLAINING WITH OUR MOUTHS AND START SEEKING HIM THROUGH OUR SPIRITS.**

FOLLOW THE OWNER'S MANUAL

If your car breaks down, you go to the dealership's service department. Your service representative goes to the owner's manual and reads what it says. Then he goes to the repair manual and proceeds to fix your car. You pay for the repairs and go on your way.

When we break down, what do we do? Most often we run to the telephone instead of God's throne. We run to Mom and cry on her shoulder about what happened today, or to the banker to talk about how bad business has been. God has given us His "Owner's Manual," the Bible, but we don't use it when we need it the most. If we would first run to the Lord and seek His will and His way, then we would know how to deal with the banker or our children or whatever problem or situation comes our way.

We take too lightly the spiritual concepts God has given us to help us succeed in our lives. Some of them are easy to say but hard to do; but if we want to start seeing results, we have to start *doing* them. It isn't good enough to just say, "I'll roll my work upon You, Lord. I'll commit it to You and trust it to You." No, you have to do it. Once you do it, then He will do His part to direct us toward the purpose He has in store for us. Proverbs 16:4 says:

> **MOST OFTEN WE RUN TO THE TELEPHONE INSTEAD OF GOD'S THRONE.**

The Lord has made everything [to accommodate itself and contribute] to its own end and His own purpose....

God has given us the ability to accommodate ourselves and contribute to our own end and His own purpose.

MAKE TITHING A WAY OF LIFE

For example, if we, as a body of Christ, would tithe, we would not need the government plans that we in America think we must have to survive—Social Security, Medicare, Medicaid, paid prescription plans for the elderly, Welfare, and so forth.

Many of God's people have not tithed. They have not even come close. Tithing is such a simple thing to do, but many people think, *Oh, but I can't live without that ten percent.* That is like saying, "I can't live unless I go steal," because that ten percent is not ours in the first place. We've prayed and asked God to get us our jobs. We've prayed and asked Him to get us our promotions and raises. Then, when these blessings have come, all of a sudden, we've started negotiating, saying, "I'm the one who worked hard. I'm the one who got up at 6 A.M."

What would have happened if God had started negotiating *after* Jesus was on the cross? What if He had said this: "Well now, My Son really doesn't have to die. I could send somebody else. We could go back to Pontius Pilate and get him to change his mind..."?

He could have started negotiating, but He didn't. God's Word is nonnegotiable. It starts on page 1 in Genesis and ends in Revelation. My Bible is printed in black and white. I don't see a place where I can erase something and write something else in. God didn't leave any fill-in-the-blank spaces.

So what makes us think we can negotiate with God? I know the Bible says, "Prove Me." You prove God when you say, "Okay God, now I'm going to stand on Your Word for

> **GOD'S WORD IS NONNEGOTIABLE.**

my healing. I'm going to prove that this is right." However, He says you'd better not test Him. Proving and testing are totally different acts. When people in the Old Testament tested Him, or prophesied falsely, they died. There is a consequence for testing God. So prove God, but don't test Him.

Cheryl sometimes says to me, "Honey, we're supposed to give that offering back." I look at our budget and it doesn't make sense in a natural sense, but I know beyond any shadow of doubt that my wife has heard from the Lord and we're supposed to do it. The reason I trust her judgment is that she has made tithing, giving, and her relationship with the Lord a way of life, and she is consistent in it. It bears witness in my spirit, and we give accordingly.

Now, if some stranger walks up to you and says, "The Lord said you are supposed to give me $1000," and it doesn't bear witness in your spirit, don't do it. When you are seeking God's will, you have to hear from God, not from people.

God spoke in Cheryl's heart and told her she was supposed to be Miss America. She knew what the Lord spoke to her, but it took five years for it to manifest. Many people told her she was not hearing from God. If she had listened to them and walked away when she didn't win after one, two, three, or four tries, she would have been out of God's will.

What if, after she had won, she had started to negotiate with God? She could have said, "Now, God, You told me I was going to be Miss America someday, but I really don't have to tell them all about my healing, do I?" Worse yet, she could have said, "Now, God, if I take that million dollars from that men's magazine, I'll give ten percent to you!"

The point is that your priorities must line up with God's Word for Him to bless you. Tithing is just one of God's principles that we must obey in order to be blessed. If you don't tithe, you will bring a curse upon yourself.

Failing to obey God by tithing is just one way we can bring a curse upon ourselves. You may ask, "How can I be redeemed from the curse if I don't know what the curse is?" The best way to be redeemed is to follow God's way in everything you do. So if you haven't been tithing, repent before God. Don't get into condemnation and guilt; just start giving at least ten percent.

There is no way in heaven and earth that you can out-give God. Commit your finances to Him and don't try to figure out how that ten percent will come from an already stretched budget. God says, "You have to trust Me with it!"

I'll be honest with you, it was hard for me to get into tithing at first. The Lord impressed on me how important it was when He said, *Someday you will be standing before Me. You told Me you gave your tenth. It's only between you and Me, not the guy sitting next to you or the guy*

> **THERE IS NO WAY IN HEAVEN AND EARTH THAT YOU CAN OUT-GIVE GOD.**

sitting behind you. You know how much you make, and you know how much the tenth is. You're telling everybody you're doing it, and one of these days you're going to have to tell Me why you didn't. I repented and changed my attitude right then and there. The biggest problem I had after that was making up the ten percent that I figured I had already robbed from God.

I share this story to let you know that none of us is perfect. We are seeking God's will, just as you are. In the process, the Lord has given us five questions that, if we can answer yes to, we can feel confident we are moving in the direction of God's will for our lives.

(1) *Does It Glorify God?*

If you want to know if you are following God's will in whatever you are seeking or doing, first ask yourself, "Is Jesus, am I, or is someone else lifted up?"

In other words, examine your motives and determine whether it is good for the kingdom of God. John 12:32 NKJV says, "And I, if I am lifted up from the earth, will draw all peoples to Myself."

Don't just read the Word every so often and expect to grow in God, because you won't. You can't know God's will without knowing God's way. His way is perfect and pure. The Word judges the thoughts and purposes of your heart. It judges your motives. Sometimes you don't even know your motive, but God does. His Word will reveal your true motive.

(2) *Does It Agree With the Word?*

Does this thing you are doing pass the Word test? Hebrews 4:12 says:

> *For the Word that God speaks is alive and full of power [making it active, operative, energizing and effective]; it is sharper than any two-edged sword, penetrating to the dividing line of the breath of life (soul) and [the immortal] spirit, and of joints and marrow [of the deepest parts of our nature], exposing and sifting and analyzing and judging the very thoughts and purposes of the heart.*

That is why the Word of God is so important to you every day, all day long. Every minute you can, get the Word inside of you and keep it in front of you. Tie it around your neck; put it in front of your face. Write it on the wall or on the mirror. Look at the Word, read the Word, and study the Word. Let your spirit become so one with it that you have to ask, "Is this my thought, or is this the Holy Spirit?"

The Word is so sharp that it can divide between the soul and the spirit. The soul is where your thought life is—your mind, your emotions. The spirit is where God's Spirit is. Sometimes when you love God and walk close to Him, the soul and spirit are so very close that it is hard to find out what the difference is. The Word of God will pierce right between the two, and you'll know. The Word will tell you and bear witness to you whether it is you or God, because the Word divides between your soul and your spirit.

(3) *Does It Produce Peace?*

If you go with whatever you're thinking, does it produce peace? Colossians 3:15 says:

> *And let the peace (soul harmony which comes) from Christ rule (act as umpire continually) in your hearts [deciding and settling with finality all questions that arise in your minds, in that peaceful state] to which as [members of Christ's] one body you were also called [to live].*

You were called to live in that peaceful state. You were called to live in the will of God. So let the peace—the soul harmony—which comes from Christ, rule or act as an umpire continually in your heart.

Can't you just see God Himself in an umpire uniform, representing peace, standing at the plate, calling the balls and the strikes? So many times we are trying to bat and call the strikes and the balls all at the same time. If you do that, then you will tend to be more favorable to yourself; you will keep yourself out of God's will many times, because you won't call it the way God would call it.

> **CAN'T YOU JUST SEE GOD HIMSELF IN AN UMPIRE UNIFORM, REPRESENTING PEACE, STANDING AT THE PLATE, CALLING THE BALLS AND THE STRIKES?**

Finding peace when making an important decision is difficult for most of us. We wrestle with it until we lose sleep and get a headache. Sometimes we get an ill feeling inside our stomachs and make excuses, saying we must have eaten something that made us nauseated.

When turmoil is ruling, it isn't God's will. The peace of God should be your ruler when any major decision or problem is before you. If you have done all the things we've talked about and have a peaceful feeling in your spirit, you can be assured it is of God.

Cheryl and I struggled during the first four or five years of our ministry over the decision to do our own TV show. Many people tried to tell us we should move ahead, but we just didn't have peace about it. We waited until we both had confirmation that it was time to move ahead. Our show is now in production and doing very well. I tried to move ahead with it a year or so earlier but just couldn't seem to make anything happen, and now I know now it wasn't God's timing right then.

Through this experience and many others like it, we have discovered how important it is for spouses to be in unity for important decisions. One spouse can act as a check and balance for the other. You have to trust each other to hear from God. If you are believing and trusting God completely with a situation, you have to trust Him to speak to your spouse as well.

Sometimes you will have to die to yourself, lose your selfish identity, to do so.

Do you know why Jacob had to wrestle with the Angel of God—Jesus? The struggle was over losing his identity. He had to take on a new identity. When we die to self, many times we wrestle and fight it because we don't want to lose our identity. I don't know why we want to keep that old junk, but we do. It's like an old shirt that is faded and threadbare, but we don't want to throw it away because it feels so comfortable.

In the early years of our marriage, Cheryl and I struggled with finding unity in making decisions regarding the balance of ministry and family. We were both doing our own things for God, but that often put us at odds with each other. God had to work on both of us to bring us to the place where we are today. When we both surrendered to the Lord, we came into unity with Him and with each other.

Dying to self brings surrender to God's will and peace to your spirit. As children we used to wrestle until someone cried, "Uncle!" That meant, "Okay, I've had enough. I quit!" And peace soon followed. Jacob struggled until his hip was out of joint and, perhaps, he cried, "Uncle!" It was a sign that he had died to self, and peace came to him.

Sometimes we bear a few scars from our struggles, but it is good to be reminded where we have been and what we have learned. Cheryl still has scars on her face from the car accident, but she bears them proudly. Perhaps it is time for you to cry "Uncle!" and quit struggling with the Lord. That's when you will find God's perfect will and His perfect peace in your life.

(4) *Does Your Spirit and God's Spirit Bear Witness Together?*

When the Holy Spirit spoke to Cheryl and said, *I want you to be in pageants, and We (the Father, Son, and Holy Spirit) will be glorified through this,* she received it in her spirit. Everybody else said, "You are missing God. You are being worldly. You are thinking wrong thoughts." She listened to what they were saying and then took it to the Lord and said, "Lord, am I?" (It's not wrong to listen and then take it to the Lord and ask. Just be sure to act on His answer.) Whenever she asked, the Holy Spirit confirmed what she was to do, and it bore witness in her spirit again and again. It was in her "knower."

When you seek God's will, it is critical that His Spirit bear witness with your spirit that it is right. How does that happen? When you die to self and surrender to the Holy Spirit, according to the Word of God, here is what happens:

> *But you are not living the life of the flesh, you are living the life of the Spirit, if the [Holy] Spirit of God [really] dwells within you [directs and controls you].... But if Christ lives in you, [then although] your [natural] body is dead by reason of sin and guilt, the spirit is alive because of [the] righteousness [that He imputes to you].*
>
> **Romans 8:9,10**

If you are alive in Christ and have the Holy Spirit living inside of you, then your spirit is in tune with the Holy Spirit and the two can bear witness with each other. Romans 8:16 says:

> *The Spirit Himself [thus] testifies together with our own spirit, [assuring us] that we are children of God.*

That means His Spirit will testify to your spirit and you will get in agreement with Him. Then you'll know that you have heard from God. It won't be something you know in your mind or your thoughts. It will be in your spirit, your heart.

(5) *Does It Pass the Test of Time?*

If you are asking yourself, "Is it God or is it me?" the way to find out is to wait and see. If it is God, it will pass the test of time. Every vision or dream has an appointed time, as Habakkuk 2:3 says:

> *For the vision is yet for an appointed time and it hastens to the end [fulfillment]; it will not deceive or disappoint. Though it tarry, wait [earnestly] for it, because it will surely come; it will not be behindhand on its appointed day.*

If you just *think* it is God, then you need to wait. If it is God, it will pass the test of time. Cheryl entered her first pageant at seventeen years old, but it was five years before she wore the Miss America crown. God's plan passed the test of time.

After her car accident at eleven years old, Cheryl wore an eighty-pound body cast for three months. She looked up at the ceiling and asked God to heal her and believed that He already had. She had no one to encourage her in her faith. Three months later, the doctors documented with x-rays a bone forming out of nothing. It wrapped all around all those pulverized, crushed pieces of bone and formed a brand new bone. The doctors wrote "miracle" on her chart. God's promise to be her healer passed the test of time.

When Cheryl went through depression our family went through hell for two years, but we firmly believe that it was part of the will of God. He didn't put the depression on us, but He saw us through it. The changes God made in Cheryl and me during that trial prepared us to launch the family ministry that we have today. God's plan passed the test of time.

We can say to you today, "It doesn't matter if you've been crippled in a car accident. It doesn't matter if you've been sexually abused. It doesn't matter if your father died when you were a child. It doesn't matter if you struggled through depression. It doesn't matter if your precious, six-year-old daughter graduated to heaven ahead of you. No matter what has happened in your life, God has a plan for you, a destiny for you to fulfill for His kingdom in His appointed time."

> **NO MATTER WHAT HAS HAPPENED IN YOUR LIFE, GOD HAS A PLAN FOR YOU, A DESTINY FOR YOU TO FULFILL FOR HIS KINGDOM IN HIS APPOINTED TIME.**

If you do what His Word says and stay in His will, He will see you through it. He will see you past it. He will see you over the top of it. Best of all, when you go over the finish line, you get to rule and reign with the King of kings and the Lord of lords.

DESTINY KEYS:

1. Identify circumstances in which you need to apply the three-step formula for counteracting the distraction.

2. Select one situation and practice rolling it onto the Lord, committing it to Him and trusting Him.

3. Apply the five questions on seeking God's will to the situation you identified above.

4. Make a decision today to seek God first regarding His will for your life.

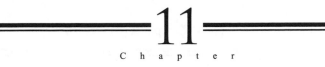

CATCH THE VISION OF YOUR DESTINY

BY CHERYL

H ave you caught the vision of your destiny yet? We have explored eight ways in which you may be distracted from your destiny and then introduced a distraction-buster formula that shows you how to find the will of God for your life and take action once you find it. However, until you catch the vision of your destiny, you will never move beyond where you are at this very moment. God has a plan and a purpose for your life, and the Holy Spirit will put the vision for your destiny in your spirit and an unstoppable dream in your heart. Prayer is the key to catching the vision of your destiny.

Jesus gave us a pattern to follow in what we call "The Lord's Prayer." He also provided a living example of a person of genuine prayer. He often went aside in the early morning hours to pray. The greatest men and women of the Bible—Moses, Hannah, Esther, David, Daniel, and Paul, just to name a few—were prayer warriors.

> **THE HOLY SPIRIT WILL PUT THE VISION FOR YOUR DESTINY IN YOUR SPIRIT AND AN UNSTOPPABLE DREAM IN YOUR HEART. PRAYER IS THE KEY TO CATCHING THE VISION OF YOUR DESTINY.**

ARE YOU LISTENING?

Here is an interesting note. The book of Exodus only speaks of Moses' praying twice. All the rest of the time God was speaking to Moses, a wise man who didn't try to do all the talking (as we so often do). Many people fail to understand that prayer is two-way communication. God wants us to talk to Him and to ask for what we need, but He also expects us to listen for His answer and His direction.

If you don't already have a daily prayer time, I urge you to make it a priority. Don't try to do it all at once. Just start with five or ten minutes and build from there. God will honor your commitment, and you will be surprised how getting into His presence increases your hunger for more of Him. It becomes easier as each day passes, so don't get under condemnation if you miss a day. It happens to all of us. The important thing is to get right back to it today, because prayer will take you to your destiny.

IGNITING AN UNSTOPPABLE DREAM

When your spirit catches the vision of your destiny, your heart ignites the passion of an unstoppable dream to take you farther and higher than you ever imagined and to do what only God makes possible.

> **WHEN YOUR SPIRIT CATCHES THE VISION OF YOUR DESTINY, YOUR HEART IGNITES THE PASSION OF AN UNSTOPPABLE DREAM TO TAKE YOU FARTHER AND HIGHER THAN YOU EVER IMAGINED AND TO DO WHAT ONLY GOD MAKES POSSIBLE.**

You may be asking, "What is an unstoppable dream?" It is one that God has planted in your heart that refuses to die or be forgotten. Sometimes it comes as a burning desire, and other times it may be something you actually dream while you are asleep. It may be a recurring dream that comes to you more than once and over time remains as fresh and clear as the day it was planted in your heart and soul. Most often it is something that is bigger than life; in other words, it seems impossible for you to accomplish or attain with your own natural abilities. An unstoppable dream requires wisdom regarding its interpretation, intent, and timing as well as discernment regarding with whom it should be shared.

The Scriptures are filled with examples of unstoppable dreams, but one of the most memorable occurs in the life story of Joseph, the favored son of Jacob. Joseph had an unstoppable dream when he was only a young teenager, and he shared it with his older brothers, who were extremely jealous of him.

Listen now and hear, I pray you, this dream that I have dreamed: We [brothers] were binding sheaves in the field, and behold, my sheaf arose and stood upright, and behold, your sheaves stood round about my sheaf and bowed down! His brothers said to him, Shall you indeed reign over us? Or are you going to have us as your subjects and dominate us? And they hated him all the more for his dreams and for what he said.

But Joseph dreamed yet another dream and told it to his brothers [also]. He said, See here, I have dreamed again, and behold, [this time not only] eleven stars [but also] the sun and the moon bowed down and did reverence to me! And he told it to his father [as well as] his brethren. But his father rebuked him and said to him, What is the meaning of this dream that you have dreamed? Shall I and your mother and your brothers actually come to bow down ourselves to the earth and do homage to you? Joseph's brothers envied him and were jealous of him, but his father observed the saying and pondered over it.

Genesis 37:6-11

Joseph's brothers hated him so much that they conspired to kill him. However, because God's hand was upon Joseph, they sold him to a band of slave traders instead and told their father that Joseph had been eaten by a wild animal.

GOD'S FAVOR PREVAILED

Joseph was too young and immature to understand the significance of this dream or his destiny, but God had a plan and a purpose that would play out over a period of thirteen years. The slave traders sold Joseph to a wealthy officer in Pharaoh's army in Egypt. God's favor went with him, and Potiphar placed Joseph in a responsible position as supervisor over his entire household. Then Potiphar's wife falsely accused Joseph of rape, and he was sent to prison.

The prison warden showed Joseph favor and placed him in charge of all of the other prisoners, including the chief of Pharaoh's bakers and the chief of his butlers. Joseph had the opportunity to interpret dreams that each of these men had on the same night while in prison. The dreams were fulfilled exactly as Joseph had interpreted them, but it was two years later before the butler had reason to remember Joseph: Pharaoh had two dreams that needed interpretation.

Pharaoh summoned Joseph from a prison dungeon and asked him to interpret the dreams. These are the words Joseph spoke to Pharaoh:

> *It is not in me; God [not I] will give Pharaoh a [favorable] answer of peace.*
>
> **Genesis 41:16**

Joseph had an excellent spirit. He went from the home of a wealthy officer to a prison pit, to the palace of Pharaoh, but he was not angry or wallowing in self-pity. He was humble and always careful to give God all of the glory for whatever favor was shown to him. After listening carefully to Pharaoh's summary of his dreams, Joseph proceeded with this interpretation:

The [two] dreams are one; God has shown Pharaoh what He is about to do. The seven good cows are seven years and the seven good ears [of grain] are seven years; the [two] dreams are one [in their meaning]. And the seven thin and ill favored cows that came up after them are seven years, and also the seven empty ears [of grain], blighted and shriveled by the east wind; they are seven years of hunger and famine. This is the message just as I have told Pharaoh; God has shown Pharaoh what He is about to do. Take note! Seven years of great plenty throughout all the land of Egypt are coming. Then there will come seven years of hunger and famine, and [there will be so much want that] all the great abundance of the previous years will be forgotten in the land of Egypt; and hunger (destitution, starvation) will exhaust (consume, finish) the land. And the plenty will become quite unknown in the land because of that following famine, for it will be very woefully severe. That the dream was sent twice to Pharaoh and in two forms indicates that this thing which God will very soon bring to pass is fully prepared and established by God. So now let Pharaoh seek out and provide a man discreet, under-standing, proficient, and wise and set him over the land of Egypt [as governor]. Let Pharaoh do this; then let him select and appoint officers over the land, and take one-fifth [of the produce] of the [whole] land of Egypt in the seven plenteous years [year by year]. And let them gather all the food of these good years that are coming and lay up grain under the direction and authority of Pharaoh, and let them retain food [in fortified granaries] in the cities. And that food shall be put in store for the country against the seven years of hunger and famine that are to come upon the land of Egypt, so that the land may not be ruined and cut off by the famine. And the plan seemed good in the eyes of Pharaoh and of all his servants.

Genesis 41:25-37

God gave Joseph the interpretation of the dream *and* a plan to deal with what was coming.

God knew what it would take to fulfill the unstoppable dream He had given to Joseph years earlier when he was still living with his father and brothers. Pharaoh named Joseph governor over his entire kingdom, and everything happened exactly as Joseph's interpretations from God had predicted.

The years of plenty were followed by years of famine, and people from other countries came to Egypt to buy grain. Jacob sent his sons to Egypt to buy grain for their families; they bowed before the governor of Egypt, though they did not recognize Joseph, just as Joseph had dreamed so many years before. Not even slavery, prison, or famine could prevent God's unstoppable dream from being fulfilled in Joseph's life.

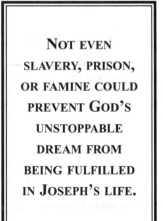

NOT EVEN SLAVERY, PRISON, OR FAMINE COULD PREVENT GOD'S UNSTOPPABLE DREAM FROM BEING FULFILLED IN JOSEPH'S LIFE.

When Joseph finally revealed his identity to his brothers they were afraid, but here is what he said.

...I am Joseph your brother, whom you sold into Egypt! But now, do not be distressed and disheartened or vexed and angry with yourselves because you sold me here, for God sent me ahead of you to preserve

life. For these two years the famine has been in the land, and there are still five years more in which there will be neither plowing nor harvest. God sent me before you to preserve for you posterity and to continue a remnant on the earth, to save your lives by a great escape and save for you many survivors. So now it was not you who sent me here, but God; and He has made me a father to Pharaoh and lord of all his house and ruler over all the land of Egypt.

Genesis 45:4-8

God knows the beginning from the end. He thinks in terms of eternity, not the here and now. He turned what appeared to be an evil plot against a young boy into a great escape from a terrible famine for the people of Israel. Joseph hadn't understood the dream he'd had as a young boy, but he had never forgotten about it. He wept when it was fulfilled and he understood the grace and mercy God had shown to his family and him.

When God puts an unstoppable dream in your heart, no one can sidetrack it but you. Joseph kept his attitude right before the Lord and didn't allow anger or bitterness to poison him. He was patient and didn't try to make anything happen by his own hand. He was a man who had a vision of his destiny and kept it before his eyes whether he was in prison or in the palace.

WHEN GOD PUTS AN UNSTOPPABLE DREAM IN YOUR HEART, NO ONE CAN SIDETRACK IT BUT YOU.

Whenever you have a God-given dream or desire, there is a threshold to be crossed and certain questions to be answered. You will ask yourself, "Am

I worthy and sufficient to fulfill this dream?" Your answer must be, "Through the blood of Jesus Christ, I am worthy; and through the power of the Spirit of the living God, I am able."

QUIT WAITING ON GOD

This is the next question: "Is this really what God wants?" When I believe that I have a dream in my heart from God, I pray, "You'd better tell me no if this isn't You, God, because I feel it in my heart and I'm going to do it unless You tell me otherwise."

Too many people sit around waiting on God while life passes them by. Quit waiting on God to write it on the wall, as He did for Belshazzar. When He plants a dream in your heart, it should be proof enough for you. You must envision your dream as a reality and embrace the victory.

Recently on the History Channel, I saw a program about massive storms. It told the story of an avalanche that buried a ski resort in the Sierra Mountains in 1982. A young woman who was a member of the ski patrol at the resort was buried alive under a mountain of snow in the employees' locker room for five days. She was the only person found alive, and she said it was her faith in God that kept her going through those grueling five days with no food or water. She suffered severe frostbite, which resulted in the amputation of one leg just below the knee and of the toes on her other foot.

She envisioned herself skiing again and persevered through the pain and negative reports from the doctors who said she would never ski again. One year later she was back on the ski slopes skiing with a prosthetic leg. Today she is the mother of two, still enjoys skiing and being active, and acknowledges that God had a plan for her life that didn't include being crippled. She embraced her victory and gave God the glory.

When I was five years old, the milkman told me I was going to be Miss America. He planted a seed in my heart. I saw myself walking that runway, waving to the crowd. I saw myself with the crown on my head. I envisioned the reality of it. I could see it in my mind and feel it in my spirit years before it ever happened. Don't let Satan come along and try to steal your vision. He doesn't want you to see it, and he will try to defeat your victory with doubt and unbelief. Don't let him do it.

ENVISION YOUR DREAM

Your dream may be for your marriage to be restored with peace and harmony. Envision it. Dream it and think it into reality. You will never act like it unless you do. If you start envisioning it, dreaming it, and acting like it, you may be amazed at what God will do. He may change *you* in ways that will draw your spouse back to you and to God.

My sister-in-law, Lindsay Roberts, and I were both told we would never be able to have children. Satan tried to steal our future children because he knew that we would empower them with the Holy Spirit and that the anointing of God would rest on every one of them. He hated the fact that our children would be taught of the Lord and that their peace and composure would be great. However, he was no match for two of the most stubborn, persevering, determined women of faith on this earth. We envisioned our dream of children and never gave up.

Lindsay gave baby showers for other women so she could envision her own dream. She sat through baby shower after baby shower envisioning herself sitting there opening presents. In our minds' eyes we saw our children running around.

If you can't envision it, you can't have it. We envisioned our children into reality. Now I see my children growing up and preaching from the platform. Harry III and Roman like nothing better than to get the microphone into their hands and go to preaching and singing. If you plant it in them, it will come up.

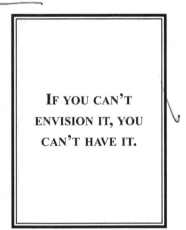

> **IF YOU CAN'T ENVISION IT, YOU CAN'T HAVE IT.**

God is speaking dreams into your heart right now. Some of you have had dreams planted for years and years. You may have let them wither and go away, but they are still there in your heart. Ask God to resurrect them and bring them back to your memory. Start envisioning them into reality. It is never too late.

APPLY THREE STEPS

What makes a dream outlive the time it takes to realize it and overcome the obstacles that stand in its way? Dreams from God are in the heart. You need to be fully conscious of them and keep them alive in your spirit no matter how long it takes them to be fulfilled.

Joseph's life was an example of how a dream can be unstoppable. He waited thirteen years to stand before Pharaoh, and at times it must have looked as though the whole world was against him. He understood the three steps to the fulfillment of an unstoppable dream:

> **DREAMS FROM GOD ARE IN THE HEART. YOU NEED TO BE FULLY CONSCIOUS OF THEM AND KEEP THEM ALIVE IN YOUR SPIRIT NO MATTER HOW LONG IT TAKES THEM TO BE FULFILLED.**

(1) He was a dreamer and spoke his dream out of his mouth.

(2) He believed it for as long as it took.

(3) He saw the fulfillment of his dream.

These three steps are clearly defined in Scripture. Let me show you in Mark 11:23,24:

> *Truly I tell you, whoever says to this mountain, Be lifted up and thrown into the sea!* [Step 1] *and does not doubt at all in his heart but believes that what he says will take place* [Step 2], *it will be done for him.* [Step 3]

> *For this reason I am telling you, whatever you ask for in prayer* [Step 1], *believe (trust and be confident) that it is granted to you* [Step 2], *and you will [get it].* [Step 3]

You can apply these three steps to your own dreams. First, pray and ask the Lord to give you a vision of your destiny; once He puts a dream in your heart, envision the reality of it. Second, believe God for it without doubting for as long as it takes, no matter what you have to go through. Third, walk out the fulfillment of the dream by embracing the victory.

When I look back at my own life, I don't focus on all the difficult tests and trials I have endured—the car accident, being sexually molested as a child, the miscarriage of our third son, being told our fourth child had miscarried and then going through a difficult pregnancy in bed for seven months, Gabrielle's being diagnosed with an inoperable brain tumor and then graduating to heaven eleven months later, being diagnosed with colon cancer only three months after Gabrielle's home-going. Instead, I thank God for how He has used these challenges to bring me to the fulfillment of my destiny to come to Jesus and to bring as many others as possible to Him.

GOD'S SOVEREIGNTY GUARANTEES FULFILLMENT

Only one word describes what makes a dream unstoppable. That word is *sovereignty.* It is the sovereignty of God that takes a girl from Choctaw County, Mississippi, and makes her Miss America. It is the sovereignty of God that takes a crushed leg and puts a new bone in it. It takes the sovereignty of God to take a face that has gone through two windshields, had over 150 stitches in it and never had plastic surgery, and make the bearer of that face Miss America. It is the sovereignty of God to take a womb like Lindsay's and mine and put baby after baby inside. It is the sovereignty of God that gives the devil one black eye, two black eyes, and a punch in the stomach.

> **ONLY ONE WORD DESCRIBES WHAT MAKES A DREAM UNSTOPPABLE. THAT WORD IS *SOVEREIGNTY.***

The sustenance and duration of your dream, or godly desire, is determined by its origin. The dream Joseph had in his heart was not first his dream. It was first God's dream. I submit to you that the dream in your heart was not first your dream. It was first God's dream, and He planted it in you. On the basis of Philippians 2:13 (NKJV) I declare to you that every godly desire you have is not yours first, because "it is God Who works in you both to will and to do for His good pleasure."

YOU CAN'T OUTRUN GOD

When God puts an unstoppable dream in your heart, nothing can take it away. Discouragement won't make it go away. You can get mad about it, try to run from it, turn away, and say, "God, I am not doing it." It still won't go away, because you didn't come up with it. God did.

Jonah found out he couldn't run away from God's unstoppable dream for him to preach repentance and save the people of Nineveh. When he tried, he ended up in the belly of a whale for three days and nights, crying out to God in repentance for his own disobedience. God had the whale vomit Jonah out onto dry land, and He spoke the dream to Jonah a second time.

This time, when Jonah was obedient, God performed a miracle. The first day Jonah entered the city of Nineveh and cried out for repentance, the people believed God and fasted and prayed for God's deliverance. The king of Nineveh got word of it, and he repented as well and declared that every man and beast would fast and pray for God's deliverance. God heard their prayers and saw their hearts, revoked His sentence, and spared the city and its inhabitants from destruction.

GOD USES IMPERFECT VESSELS

An unstoppable dream will outlive your discouragement. It will outlive the obstacles that stand in its way. It will even outlive your anger and pity-parties.

God proved that to Jonah. After the people of Nineveh repented before God, Jonah was angry. His pride was hurt because he thought the people deserved to be judged for their wickedness. He went outside the city and had a major pity-party all by himself. His anger was so intense that he prayed to die. God rebuked him and showed him how misplaced his anger was. God's mercy and grace were greater than Jonah's anger and pity-party because it was God's dream to save Nineveh, not Jonah's. Jonah was simply the imperfect vessel God used to make it happen.

Joseph had a dream, and all hell broke loose in his life. Calamity was on every hand. The dreamer who had the dream looked to the casual observer as if he were going away from the fulfillment of the dream. Joseph's dream was bigger than Joseph.

Your dream is bigger than you. I want you to get a hold of that. It is God's dream. You may feel as if you are going away from your dream, but you're not. You are headed toward it all the time.

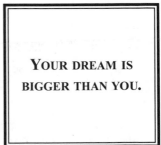

YOUR DREAM IS BIGGER THAN YOU.

195

START *BECOMING* YOUR DREAM

God does several things after you catch the dream—the vision of your destiny. First, He begins to work *for* you. The second thing He does is to work *on* you.

For God to fulfill the dream, He has to work on you. The person who walks in the fulfillment of the dream is not the same person who dreamed the dream. The girl who walked down that runway as Miss America and gave God all the glory is not the same girl who dreamed the dream. It may be the same body, but the person inside changes along the way. God gives the dream, and then the person starts *becoming* the dream.

> **THE PERSON WHO WALKS IN THE FULFILLMENT OF THE DREAM IS NOT THE SAME PERSON WHO DREAMED THE DREAM.**

That is why the timing has to be perfect. What happened between the time Joseph dreamed his dream and the time he stood before Pharaoh? He was becoming the dream. The Joseph who stood before Pharaoh was not the same Joseph who stood before his brothers, because God changed him in the meantime. The Joseph who stood before his brothers could dream the dream, but the Joseph who stood before Pharaoh could fulfill the dream. Between the Joseph who dreamed and the Joseph who walked in the fulfillment of the dream was a God big enough to enable Joseph to take everything that came his way and use it for God's glory and Joseph's good.

Joseph's life is proof that adversities, misunderstandings, mistreatment, and hurdles cannot stop the dream. You are the only one who can stop your dream at any point, but if you will allow God to work for you and on you, He will take trials and make them transportation to take you right to your destination. God will take adversities and make them advantages. He will take persecution and turn it into perseverance in you. He will take hurdles and make them into halos. He will take tribulations and make them treasures for you. He will take tests and make them triumphs.

Everything you walk through is taking you to your dream. The dream of God in you is unstoppable because God doesn't just give you the dream and leave you. The Giver of the dream is the Keeper of the dream. When Joseph was sold into slavery in Egypt and went to Potiphar's house, God was with him:

THE GIVER OF THE DREAM IS THE KEEPER OF THE DREAM.

But the Lord was with Joseph, and he [though a slave] was a successful and prosperous man; and he was in the house of his master the Egyptian. And his master saw that the Lord was with him and that the Lord made all that he did to flourish and succeed in his hand.

Genesis 39:2,3

When Potiphar's wife lied and falsely accused Joseph of rape and Joseph was taken to prison, God was with him.

But the Lord was with Joseph and showed him mercy and loving-kindness and gave him favor in the sight of the warden of the prison. And the warden of the prison committed to Joseph's care all the prisoners who were in the prison; and whatsoever was done there, he was in charge of it. The prison warden paid no attention to anything that was in [Joseph's] charge, for the Lord was with him and made whatever he did to prosper.

Genesis 39:21-23

In each instance, Joseph ended up ruling. He ruled at Potiphar's house and then in the prison while he was becoming the Joseph that would one day rule all of Egypt. God was molding him, changing him, turning him into the man that could handle the fulfillment of the dream.

CHANGE IS AN EVOLVING PROCESS

> IF GOD ALLOWED YOU TO FULFILL YOUR DREAM IMMEDIATELY, YOU COULDN'T HANDLE THE DREAM BECAUSE YOU WOULDN'T BE READY FOR IT.

If God allowed you to fulfill your dream immediately, you couldn't handle the dream because you wouldn't be ready for it. God's timing is perfect, so don't get discouraged and quit or get mad at God if your dream isn't fulfilled right away.

Just let Him work on you and change you into the person He needs you to be so you can fulfill the dream. Take one step at a time. If you are faithful over a few things, He will make you ruler over many. Very few people want to be faithful over a few things, but they sure do want to be rulers over many. They want to start in business as the president, but they must learn so their business will survive more than one day.

This reminds me of some little bugs that you can see all over the trees in Mississippi. When you look at one, you see a shell and its little legs; but as you look closer, you discover it is just an empty casing that the bug outgrew and left behind.

I am not one who dreams very often at night, and my dreams seldom have any spiritual connotation. If I dream, I can rarely remember the details. However, about fourteen months after Gabrielle went to heaven, I had a significant dream. I know it was significant because it is as real to me today as it was the night I dreamed it.

In the dream Gabrielle was apparently in heaven, but the setting was rather unusual. She was in what appeared to be some type of a classroom with a dozen or more other children and two of the most beautiful women I have ever seen, dressed in gorgeous clothing. The children were beautifully dressed as well.

Knowledge was literally in the air coming at them, and they were absorbing it in their entire beings. As it flowed into them, they were getting smarter and smarter.

As the dream progressed, I tried to get Gabrielle to come to me. It wasn't as if she ignored me or said, "No, Mommy." It was as if I was a nonentity to her or as if what I was asking couldn't even penetrate her realm.

I woke up and immediately remembered every detail of the dream, which never happens with me.

I went right back to sleep and dreamed exactly the same dream again, except it was in a different location. The children and the two ladies were in school, and knowledge was coming at them from every direction. They were learning more and more right in front of my eyes. Again, I tried to get Gabrielle to come to me, but she didn't respond in any way.

I woke up again and remembered the whole dream before dropping off to sleep a third time.

I dreamed the same dream, but it was in a third location. At the end of this dream, Gabrielle said something to one of the other children, and she used the word "them" when she should have used the word "those." My teacher mentality invoked an automatic response, and I corrected her grammar. As I did so, she turned and looked at me with her piercing blue eyes and said, "The spot and wrinkle on the body of Christ are not those who need correcting. The spot and wrinkle on the body of Christ are those who are doing the correcting."

I woke up and knew God was talking to me through Gabrielle and telling me not to fall into criticism or judgment because that literally causes a spot and wrinkle on the body of Christ. I have pondered this dream repeatedly, and every time I start to make a statement about someone, I think of what Gabrielle said. I don't want to be a spot or a wrinkle, because Jesus is coming for a spotless church without wrinkles. I am still in the process of *becoming* what God wants me to be.

When you get a dream from God, you keep outgrowing your casing. Everything that happens between you and the fulfillment of your dream causes you to keep outgrowing your casing. You go through a test and get bigger than that casing. Next, you go through a trial and get bigger than that casing. You keep growing to the next size and then outgrow that one. That is how God evolves you and changes you.

All of a sudden you are overcoming every obstacle and are looking back at each one, wondering how you got over it. You may not know how you got over it, but you know who got you over. It was not Potiphar or the prison warden that promoted Joseph and made him ruler. God was setting Joseph up, training him, teaching him, molding him into what He needed him to be, so the dream could be fulfilled in his life.

BE ENCOURAGED

When the tests and the trials and disappointments come, if you have a dream from God, you also have the God of the dream. He won't leave you. When you start talking about your dream, you start becoming the dream. Between the dream and the season in which you walk in its fulfillment, you become what God has called and predestined you to be.

> WHEN THE TESTS AND THE TRIALS AND DISAPPOINTMENTS COME, IF YOU HAVE A DREAM FROM GOD, YOU ALSO HAVE THE GOD OF THE DREAM.

When adversity or persecution comes from others, be encouraged. You don't have to even the score. The day will come when, just like Joseph, you will be able to look your wrongdoers right in the eye and say, "You may have intended it for evil, but God intended it for my good. I am here to serve God and to help you."

You can't stop people from talking, but you can stop their talking from stopping you. They can't kill your dream. All you have to do is just keep dreaming the dream and walking with the One who gave you the dream. Stand firm on this Scripture:

> **YOU CAN'T STOP PEOPLE FROM TALKING, BUT YOU CAN STOP THEIR TALKING FROM STOPPING YOU.**

Who shall ever separate us from Christ's love? Shall suffering and affliction and tribulation? Or calamity and distress? Or persecution or hunger or destitution or peril or sword? Even as it is written, For Thy sake we are put to death all the day long; we are regarded and counted as sheep for the slaughter. Yet amid all these things we are more than conquerors and gain a surpassing victory through Him Who loved us.

Romans 8:35-37

Nothing and no one can separate us from the love of God. Joseph and God were inseparable. No one could separate them. God and you are inseparable. Nobody can separate you from God or from His love.

In the early church, the apostles were persecuted and even thrown into prison for preaching about Jesus. The religious leaders of their day were jealous of the attention the people gave them. Acts 5 says that Peter and the apostles were put in jail and an angel of the Lord came in the night, led them out of the prison, and said:

> *Go, take your stand in the temple courts and declare to the people the whole doctrine concerning this Life (the eternal life which Christ revealed).*

Acts 5:20

The apostles had a clear vision of their destiny. God had given them a dream, and no one could stop them from fulfilling it. They were brought before the Sanhedrin, the temple council, and even the high priest couldn't stop them from preaching the Good News. Then Gamaliel, one of the most respected teachers of the Law spoke up and said:

> *"And now I say to you, keep away from these men and let them alone; for if this plan or this work is of men, it will come to nothing; but if it is of God, you cannot overthrow it—lest you even be found to fight against God."*

Acts 5:38,39 NKJV

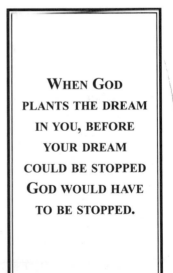

WHEN GOD PLANTS THE DREAM IN YOU, BEFORE YOUR DREAM COULD BE STOPPED GOD WOULD HAVE TO BE STOPPED.

What is the source of your dream? If you can honestly say God is the source, I'm telling you that your dream is unstoppable. Nothing on earth or in hell can stop your dream's fulfillment. When God plants the dream in you, before your dream could be stopped God would have to be stopped. Have you ever heard of anything or anybody big enough to stop God? There isn't one.

YOUR DREAM IS FIRMLY ESTABLISHED

There may be times when you wonder, *Will this ever happen?* Don't you think Joseph wondered that a few times in those thirteen years?

Nevertheless, don't be tempted to take matters into your own hands and try to make it happen. When Joseph stood before Pharaoh, who had a dream, there was a relationship between Joseph's dream and Pharaoh's dream. Pharaoh had a dream and then had another dream. As Joseph interpreted the two dreams, he said to Pharaoh:

> *That the dream was sent twice to Pharaoh and in two forms indicates that this thing which God will very soon bring to pass is fully prepared and established by God.*

> **Genesis 41:32**

In other words, Joseph was saying, "You have had this same dream twice. And the reason you've dreamed it twice is that the matter is firmly established by God. It is not your dream. It was God showing you what He is about to do."

How many times did Joseph have his dream? Two. When God put those words in Joseph's mouth and he spoke them aloud to Pharaoh, can't you just imagine something going "click" in his mind? His memories must have taken him back thirteen years to the dream of the sheaves and then of the sun and the moon and the eleven stars bowing down to him. Don't you know he must have been thinking, *I'm standing here about to see the fulfillment of my dream?*

When I was on that runway in Atlantic City in 1980 with that crown on my head and my hands lifted up, giving God all the glory because He had delivered me from sexual abuse and from being crippled and scarred, nobody could have kept my hands down. Nobody could have kept the praise off my lips. Nobody could have kept me from saying that God is a big God, a good God. He can find you anywhere and turn you into anything. He can do anything in your life. Nobody could stop me from saying that because when I stood on that runway, I realized that the fulfillment of my dream was there and I was walking in it.

When you have waited so long for your dream, you hardly know how to act when it gets there. It comes on you so quickly that you don't know how to quit believing for it and start walking in it. But trust me, it just comes naturally. All of a sudden, you can just walk right in it.

Be encouraged. When the dream is God's, it will outlive your frustration. It will outlive your discouragement. It will live beyond every adversity. You may forget about it for a while. You may just give it up and walk away from it. But there shall come a time, if you walk on with God, when you'll remember that God gave the dream and, just as surely as He gave it, He has brought it to pass.

What makes the dream unstoppable? The sovereignty of God is what makes the impossible possible.

For with God nothing is ever impossible and no word from God shall be without power or impossible of fulfillment.

Luke 1:37

According to this Word, it is impossible for you not to fulfill your dream. Get it past your head and into your heart that the dream God planted in you is unstoppable. It is impossible for it to fail. It is impossible for you not to accomplish it. It is impossible for you not to walk in the fulfillment of it. It is your dream, given by God. It was His dream first, and His Word doesn't fail or return void, because the Giver of the dream is the Keeper of the dream. It is impossible for that dream not to come into fulfillment.

> **GET IT PAST YOUR HEAD AND INTO YOUR HEART THAT THE DREAM GOD PLANTED IN YOU IS UNSTOPPABLE.**

You have dreams for your family. You have had dreams for your own ministry and your own life. You have had dreams for your spouse and for your children. Don't give up on them. Don't quit believing in them. Don't quit walking in your faith. They are coming in God's perfect timing. They are on their way.

When God gives a dream, the dream is sovereign. It outlives; it endures; it emerges. Between dreaming it and walking in it, you will become it. God is fulfilling your dream as He is working on you. Don't despise the *becoming* years. God stands between the person you were when you dreamed and the person you became at the dream's fulfillment. He makes everything you encounter—between dreaming and fulfillment—work together for your good because you love Him and are called according to a purpose and a dream that is beyond you.

God knew what He was doing when He planted the dream in your heart. I'm telling you, when you have a dream from God, catch the vision of your destiny and let hell come on because heaven shall prevail. If you stay with God, you will prevail because your dream is unstoppable and your destiny is fully prepared and established by God!

> **IF YOU STAY WITH GOD, YOU WILL PREVAIL BECAUSE YOUR DREAM IS UNSTOPPABLE AND YOUR DESTINY IS FULLY PREPARED AND ESTABLISHED BY GOD!**

DESTINY KEYS:

1. Establish a daily prayer time and listen for God's instruction and direction.

2. Ask the Lord to give you an unstoppable dream and a plan to fulfill it.

3. Apply the three steps of asking, believing, and walking out your dream.

4. Practice envisioning your dream.

5. Personalize this Scripture and speak it out loud:

    Who shall separate [me] from Christ's love? Shall suffering and affliction and tribulation? Or calamity and distress? Or persecution or hunger or destitution or peril or sword? Even as it is written, For Thy sake [I am] put to death all the day long; [I am] regarded and counted as a sheep for the slaughter. Yet amid all these things I am more than a conqueror and gain a surpassing victory through Him Who loved [me].

    Romans 8:35-37

RECORD AND PLANT THE VISION

BY HARRY

A re you discovering, expanding, or enlarging your vision? Perhaps you are raising a vision from the dead. No matter what stage you are in, it is critical that you not lose the vision God has put within you. Your vision is of vital importance to your life and happiness.

> *Where there is no vision [no redemptive revelation of God], the people perish; but he who keeps the law [of God, which includes that of man]—blessed (happy, fortunate, and enviable) is he.*

Proverbs 29:18

A vision from God provides you with a redemptive revelation of Him. Without that revelation, you cannot have an intimate, personal relationship with Him and you will never find true peace and happiness. That is why once you catch the vision of the unstoppable dream God has planted in your heart, you must never let it go. It is your destiny.

> **A VISION FROM GOD PROVIDES YOU WITH A REDEMPTIVE REVELATION OF HIM.**

The best way to keep your vision in front of your eyes is to write it down. God's Word tells us specifically to do this.

And the Lord answered me and said, Write the vision and engrave it so plainly upon tablets that everyone who passes may [be able to] read [it easily and quickly] as he hastens by.

Habakkuk 2:2

Did you write down the vision or unstoppable dreams God gave you when you completed the last chapter? If not, find a piece of paper or sit down at your computer and ask the Lord to bring it all back to your mind. Search your memory for any dreams you had years ago that you pushed aside as impossible. Take time right now to write down, with as much detail as possible, everything God brings to your mind.

The reason God tells us to write it down is to keep us from getting sidetracked or discouraged. The enemy will use every distraction and tactic in the world to keep you from reaching your destiny. If your vision is clearly written down, you won't forget about or be distracted from where you are headed.

In an earlier chapter, we learned that the word *vision* in the Hebrew signifies an agreement. By writing your vision down, you are making an agreement with God.

If you want to do a certain thing for God, find a place in your Bible to write it down, date it, and make an agreement with God. That way you won't back out of your agreement or change your mind when the going gets tough.

> **IF YOUR VISION IS CLEARLY WRITTEN DOWN, YOU WON'T FORGET ABOUT OR BE DISTRACTED FROM WHERE YOU ARE HEADED.**

HOLD ON AND DON'T QUIT

Cheryl sings a song that says, "Hold on, hold on, hold on." You have to hold on to your vision and dream because the devil never gets tired of being the devil. The reason he never quits or keeps coming back is that he doesn't have anything else to do but torment God's people. He keeps using every weapon in his arsenal to get you to give up on your vision and turn away from what God has called you to do.

That is why you have to dig in your heels and write your vision down as a supernatural act of God. Literally, you make a contract with God that cannot be broken.

Remember that the Giver of the dream is the Keeper of the dream.

> **YOU HAVE TO HOLD ON TO YOUR VISION AND DREAM BECAUSE THE DEVIL NEVER GETS TIRED OF BEING THE DEVIL.**

God is not finished with you yet, so don't quit and don't give up right on the brink of your miracle. He hasn't given up on you, so don't give up on Him. He has a plan and a purpose, and He will fulfill it. You don't have to figure out *how* to do it. All you have to do is pray and be obedient to *do* what He tells you to do and to *go* where He tells you to go. Roll it over on Him, commit it to Him, and trust Him, no matter how long it takes.

THE TEST OF TIME PRODUCES FAITH

We have talked quite a bit in previous chapters about the importance of God's timing, but we can never say enough about it. Every vision has an appointed time.

> *For the vision is yet for an appointed time and it hastens to the end [fulfillment]; it will not deceive or disappoint. Though it tarry, wait [earnestly] for it, because it will surely come; it will not be behindhand on its appointed day.*
>
> **Habakkuk 2:3**

Your vision will not deceive or disappoint you. It will come to fulfillment; you will get it. It is a done deal. That is God's promise, so hold on to it. Don't get anxious, because just when you think it can never happen God will complete it within you.

IF WE RECEIVED EVERYTHING WE BELIEVED FOR THE SECOND WE BELIEVED, THEN IT WOULDN'T TAKE ANY FAITH TO GET IT.

It is when a vision tarries that we get off track and lose our miracle or forget our vision and dreams. Time is a very important part of God's plan for us. It is the part that requires our faith. Without time, we wouldn't need faith. If we received everything we believed for the second we believed, then it wouldn't take any faith to get it.

When you write your vision down and come into covenant agreement with God to fulfill it, you then must have the faith to wait on His timing and remain alert to hear His voice. It doesn't matter if no one else comes into agreement with you. God is the only One you need.

DEFEAT THE GIANTS IN LIFE

When young David had a vision to take on the giant Goliath, no one else thought he could do it. The first thing they did was put someone else's armor on him. David never could have killed Goliath if he had been weighted down with Saul's heavy armor. The vision belonged to David, and no one else could do it for him. David had a bigger vision that day than anyone else did. All he had was a slingshot and five stones. He knew he needed only one shot to kill Goliath, but he was prepared to drop as many giants as necessary. There are many giants in your life. You have to expand your vision to defeat them all.

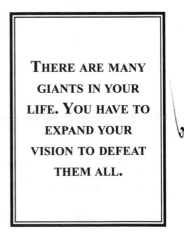

> **THERE ARE MANY GIANTS IN YOUR LIFE. YOU HAVE TO EXPAND YOUR VISION TO DEFEAT THEM ALL.**

Going through Gabrielle's sickness and Cheryl's operation for colon cancer, we almost lost our vision. Cheryl and I knew we had to go to the next level with God. He took us from the child's table to the

King's table, and we began to see higher and further than ever before. We began to expand our vision when we came to the realization that God was doing something through restoration. We discovered we had the prophetic word in our mouths for our future, and we began to shout, "Restore!" for our family, our marriage, our home, our ministry, and our vision. We shouted, "Restore! Restore! Restore!"

Then the Lord gave us this life-changing word through Pastor Jerry Barnard: "After restoration comes divine visitation." Our vision expanded dramatically when we received the revelation that something comes *after* restoration. That something is divine visitation, which brings with it an expanded vision for the future.

EXPANDING THE VISION

Our vision is to be able to fulfill all the speaking dates we haven't been able to fulfill because of the time it takes to travel from one location to another. We did it for a season traveling in our motor coach, but we just can't do it anymore. We have so many dates we cannot fulfill right now because we can't get there.

I said to Cheryl one day, "We've got to have an airplane." That's a big vision, but my ability to dream didn't start there.

When I was a kid I had a vision for a bicycle. I worked hard and believed and gave my twenty-five cents to the building fund at church every week. I got my bicycle.

Then I had a dream for an automobile. I got my automobile.

When I moved away from home, I had a dream for an apartment. I got my apartment.

I had a dream and a vision for a house, and I got my house.

I had a dream and a vision for a wife. I got "Miss America"!

God takes you toward your vision in steps to build your faith. He doesn't give you a Rolls Royce at the age of eight. With me, He started with a bicycle because I had bicycle faith.

When we first launched out in our family ministry, we needed a van, and it was a great harvest when we got it. Then God provided us a motor home, and that was a huge harvest. It was so timely and such a blessing especially when Gabrielle was so ill. We don't have it anymore because God wanted to expand our vision.

Here is how He did it. A pastor came to us and said, "You have a need to travel in another vehicle."

"Yes, we do."

"How about our motor coach? Would you like to buy it?"

"No, we don't go in debt. Our motor home is paid for, and it's good enough."

Cheryl walked out of the church and climbed up inside that motor coach. As she stepped through the door, the Holy Spirit said, *This is your motor coach!* She immediately got into agreement with Him and said, "Holy Spirit, You are right. This *is* our motor coach!"

It was 110° Fahrenheit in Dallas that day, and I said, "Cheryl, you are having a heatstroke."

"I am not. If you'll come into agreement with me, we'll have it."

"Do you know how much one of these costs?"

"I don't care how much it costs; God said it is ours. I'm not having a heatstroke; I'm having a faithstroke."

The senior pastor called us a few days later and said, "We believe you are supposed to be riding in that motor coach."

"Pastor, I'm not going in debt for it."

"Let me call you back. I think we can work something out."

To make a long story short, the pastor called us back and said, "We paid $108,000 for the motor coach, and we have paid it down to $85,000. We want to help you. Can you come up with $55,000?"

Now, that was closer to what we could handle. This wasn't a good deal; it was a God deal. We began to plant seed for that vehicle. Within ninety days we had the motor coach, and it was completely paid for. Rather than them giving it to us, we had faith for the vehicle in the first place, then exercised our faith in the midst of the blessing for the money for it.

We needed that motor coach and received it in October '98. January '99 was when Gabrielle became ill, and we utilized the motor coach that entire year to keep her medically treated while we were traveling. Without it we could not have done that.

We have learned an amazing principle of seed, faith, and harvest. What once was the greatest harvest you've ever had will become your seed for an even greater future harvest, because your harvest grows. Think of the greatest harvest you have gotten and imagine it as your seed. That is where God is taking you. This year we planted our vehicle into another ministry because God said we needed to plant transportation to harvest transportation. Our van, which was once our harvest, is now our seed!

> **WHAT ONCE WAS THE GREATEST HARVEST YOU'VE EVER HAD WILL BECOME YOUR SEED FOR AN EVEN GREATER FUTURE HARVEST, BECAUSE YOUR HARVEST GROWS.**

Do you remember the Bible story in which it took two men to carry two bunches of grapes on a pole in the land of the giants? The grapes represent the blessing. Can you imagine how big the blessings were back then? Our blessings today have to be great, too. I have great faith for an airplane. I said to Cheryl, "To do what we're called to do to expand our vision, we're going to sow everything."

ESTABLISH A STOREHOUSE

Three days earlier Cheryl and I had a very significant conversation. She said, "The Lord told me He will fill our storehouse. We have to have a storehouse. Harry, we want to share our vision about believing God for an airplane, and we don't even have a storehouse for an airplane. You need to open an account for an airplane."

You can talk about God's filling your storehouse, but do you have one for Him to fill? I went to the bank and asked what I needed to do to open an interest-bearing account. They said $2,500.00 is required for that type of account. I said, "I'll be back."

That day a $2000 check came from a man in Michigan. He wrote, "I heard you talking to your wife at lunch about your vision. (It was a private conversation.) Here is $2000 for fuel for your airplane." He wasn't even at our table, but having lunch at the same place we were. I said that if I would have known he was interested in our conversation, I would have been happy for him to pull up a chair. Another lady sent us a $10 check. She had attended the church we had given the van to and wanted to help us with our vision. Another man sent us a $500 check the same day! This was very unusual for us—$2,510 in one day!

I went to the bank and said, "I want to open up that account. I have $2,510 for our travel account."

I went home and said, "It's open. We have a storehouse with $2,510 in it."

Cheryl said, "Good. Now God will fill it. Do you agree?" The boys and I agreed right there with Cheryl.

You can't expect God to fill something you don't have. We don't believe it was coincidence that the very day we determined to open a storehouse is the day the first seed came in.

DON'T STEP BACK

That same week we went to minister in Tennessee. The Spirit of the Lord broke out in that church in a prophetic wave with a word for the pastor about going to the next level where

God wants him to be, where He wants his finances met, where He wants his wife to prosper, where He wants him to prosper.

People in ministry all stopped talking about prosperity in the late '80s when so many ministries got into the news. I believe as Christians, we took a step back.

However, Cheryl and I have decided we are not stepping back any longer. We lost too much ground. I believe we are living in the end times. The wealth of the wicked is stored up for the just. (Prov. 13:22.) We have to claim our wealth now and receive it. It's not about boats and houses and cars. It is about the abundant blessing; it's about the work we have to do. We must put our sickles to the ground for multitudes—multitudes in the valley of decision. Let me tell you, you don't travel across this nation for free. Gas costs money.

Philippians 4:12 says having enough to spare (author's paraphrase). You won't win the world with an empty hand. It is going to take feeding the hungry, clothing the poor, and housing the homeless. Abundance is having more than enough to help others, and in that you can share the love of Jesus with them.

They never took up an offering for our ministry needs at that church service, but people came with their offerings. People had received this understanding about praise and worship with finances: We don't just praise with our mouths; we can also praise with our tithes and offerings, talents, and time.

People began to come up and just lay money on the altar as an act of worshiping God. They planted into our vision because they began to realize that God gives birth to our visions when we plant in others' visions. We weren't preaching about that.

We were just prophesying to the pastor. That is when Cheryl said the provision is in the vision.

> **GOD GIVES BIRTH TO OUR VISIONS WHEN WE PLANT IN OTHERS' VISIONS.**

We shared our vision about our airplane, and that afternoon the pastor called and said, "We want to take you out to dinner. Another couple in the church wants to go with us."

We met at a restaurant and had dinner, and the other couple invited us to come to their home for dessert.

We drove up to their house, and I thought, *Jed, Ellie May, Granny, and Jethro will all be coming out the front door any minute.* It was a beautiful home.

We walked inside, and our hostess said, "Would you like a tour?" Our mouths were hanging open in awe. I thought, *Yeah, I've got three days. Start the tour.* She started the tour, and in the first room she took us to she said, "This is my wrapping room." There were many rolls of wrapping paper along the walls. There was a table, huge scissors, tape, ribbon, and a computer to print out the labels.

I had never stood in a wrapping room before, and this one room was as big as the entire house Cheryl had grown up in. It was incredible. She explained that she sent presents out all over the country.

Cheryl immediately thought, *This is a giving woman. She has a room designated for gifts. God, this woman is a giver and I want to be her friend.*

When you share your vision, there is provision in the vision. We walked out of that room and were standing in the hallway talking. Our hostess said, "What kind of airplane are you believing for?" We told her.

"Well, I got on the Internet today and looked up a few things. Here—these are for you to take home." While I was reading what she had handed me, she handed Cheryl an envelope. Cheryl opened it up, tapped me on the shoulder, and handed me a check. This was four days after we had opened our storehouse.

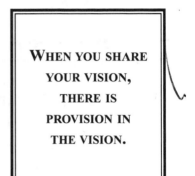

WHEN YOU SHARE YOUR VISION, THERE IS PROVISION IN THE VISION.

Our hostess said, "I want to plant into your vision with a $10,000 check for your airplane. I'm sowing into your vision for my vision." We had never met this woman or her husband before that day.

"What is your vision? Would you share it with us?"

"I'm believing for seventy billion dollars to touch the nations for Jesus. I want to help ministries that can go out and reach the world."

In my opinion, these people were "very comfortable." But that isn't enough to fulfill her vision, because she and her husband have a great *big* vision.

We left that house with our vision expanded. You need to surround yourself with people of great vision. Not people who have no vision, who desire to pull you down. Have you ever told someone you are going to get out of debt? The first thing they usually say is, "Oh, no your not. That's absurd." They are dream stealers instead of dream seekers. Choose relationships with people of vision.

DREAM SEEKERS CREATE A FUTURE

Cheryl says, "Hang around with people who have a bigger vision than yours; it will expand yours." Hang around with people with greater faith than yours. Hang around with people who are walking in the blessing, so it will get on you as you walk with them.

Don't hang with people who pat your back and say, "Bless your heart, poor thing." Hang with people who will kick you in the spiritual backside and make you straighten up.

As we said earlier, two kinds of people will come across your life: dream seekers and dream stealers. Dream stealers say, "You can't do it. You came from the wrong side of the tracks. You wore flour sack dresses. Who do you think you are?" Dream seekers say, "Little girl, one day you will be Miss America." You have to hang with the right kind of people: faith people, visionaries, and dream seekers.

As we spent time with people like this, our storehouse was growing. We went to a church in Alabama, and a man in the church came up to me and said we need insurance for the airplane we're believing for. I said, "Yes, I am." He told me he was an insurance salesman but did not sell airplane insurance. He gave me a check for $1000 to help with our first year of aviation insurance. Now we have a storehouse, fuel money, and a hangar.

We went to another church, and a woman came running out of the crowd and said, "I used to be a pilot for Kenneth Copeland. When I flew for him, I put the key to the airplane on this key ring. (It was a sterling silver key chain.) I want you to have it so that when you get your airplane you can put your key on it."

We came home and were talking with a man who is a pilot and whose life we have been sowing into. He said, "When you get your airplane, I'd like to fly you wherever you want to go, whenever you want to go. I'm going to sow that into your ministry."

Now we have a pilot, a sterling silver key chain, a hangar, fuel money, and a storehouse with money in it. Why? People are catching the vision because we are sharing it and making it plain.

A woman came up to Cheryl, handed her a watch, and said, "Here. This is so you'll be on time for the airplane."

SPECIFIC SEED PRODUCES
A SPECIFIC HARVEST

This all began when we planted transportation for a transportation harvest. God had given us our van as our miracle in the early days of our ministry. We had been believing God for our airplane but hadn't shared the vision with anybody yet. The Lord said to Cheryl, *If you want an airplane, you have to plant seed for an airplane.*

She said, "Father, if I had an airplane I would give one away, but I don't have one so I can't give it away." An airplane is transportation. If you want transportation, you've got to plant transportation.

The Lord spoke to me at the same time, and I said to Cheryl, "We need to give your van away." It was the only vehicle we had, but she said, "Okay, I agree with you. Let's pray and find out who we are supposed to give it to."

We prayed about it, and I said, "Cheryl, I know who we're supposed to give the van to." She said, "The boys and I were praying over our mail one day, and I know, too. You write it down, and I'll write it down. Then we'll swap papers and see who it is."

We looked at the name on the papers, and we both had the same name. It was the name of a young pastor in Missouri who personally busses more than 400 children to church every Tuesday night. This is in a town with approximately 1200 children in the whole school district. The very day I called him, his car, which had well over 100,000 miles on it, had quit the day before. In fertile ground, we sowed transportation for transportation.

Now we have a storehouse, money for fuel, a key chain, a pilot, a watch, and insurance. Our airplane is in the air coming toward us.

Share your vision, because the provision is in the vision. If you don't share it with others, they won't be able to sow into your vision. As you share, others will catch their own vision more easily.

DREAM BIG

God wants you to have a vision and a dream, and He doesn't want it to be small. He wants it to be big, because He is a big God. He wants you to be fulfilled, not in your flesh but in your spirit. That only happens when you seek Him first or when you call upon Him.

Habakkuk 3:2 says, "Write the vision," but first it says, "The Lord answered me and said...." God is telling you to catch your vision, write it down, share it with others, and go after it with all you've got in you. It is your destiny. It also says to engrave it. If you don't engrave it, you might change your vision because of time, discouragement, or people. Write the vision down.

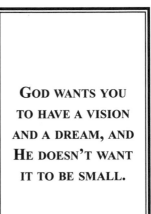

GOD WANTS YOU TO HAVE A VISION AND A DREAM, AND HE DOESN'T WANT IT TO BE SMALL.

DESTINY KEYS:

1. After you write down your vision, break it down into reasonable action steps that will take you from where you are to where you need to be.

2. Assign priorities to these steps, and set a realistic timetable for completing each one.

3. Identify any obstacles to completing these steps, and develop a plan to overcome such obstacles.

4. Develop a plan to share your vision, and write a list of those with whom you will share it.

5. Set weekly goals to accomplish each step in a reasonable manner.

6. Keep a record of your progress, no matter how small, and encourage yourself in moving forward.

CONCLUSION:
PROTECT
YOUR ASSETS

BY HARRY AND CHERYL

N ow that you know that your destiny is to come to Jesus and bring as many others with you as possible, are you ready to go into action? It doesn't matter how you get to Jesus; just get there!

Look around you. Everywhere you look, there are people who desperately need to get to Jesus and don't know how. You don't have to be a seasoned evangelist. All you have to do is invite them to come with you to church, a Bible study, or a home group meeting. If you invite them, Jesus will bring them into the fold and your pastor will shepherd them once they are there.

Have you ever seen a shepherd give birth to a sheep? Of course not! Sheep give birth to sheep. You are a sheep, so it is up to you to help bring forth a vision in someone else. You may be thinking, *I've tried that, and it doesn't work.* Well, maybe it wasn't the right time; maybe your heart wasn't totally in it; perhaps your approach wasn't quite right.

Christianity isn't about "religion." It is about *relationship* with a loving Father and with the best Friend and Brother a person could ever have. The world has seen all the religion they can stomach, but they desperately need love and acceptance.

The most important asset you have to give someone else is love. It is by loving the people of the world, not condemning them, that we bring them into God's kingdom. You may need to build a relationship with your neighbors for a time before you invite them to church or even start talking about Jesus. When they see your testimony rather than hear it, they will want what you have.

If we want to draw people to Jesus, we need to learn how to be friendly and hospitable. Gabrielle was Miss Hospitality. She lived up to her name because she loved to "gab." When the telephone rang, she was the first to reach it and issue her favorite invitation, "Ya come to my house?"

Now she is our ambassador in heaven, and you can be sure that she has the door to her mansion open wide, waiting for the multitudes from the valley of decision to come to her house. We won't disappoint her. Come hell or high water we won't quit, and we won't give up telling everyone we see about our Jesus. No matter how much it rains or how high the water rises, we stay focused on Jesus. We don't listen to the dream stealers. We hang out with the dream seekers.

This is one thing of which you can be certain: With each higher level in reaching your destiny, the devil has a new tactic to try to bring you down. You will never outgrow the devil. You have to learn to keep doing what God has called you to do and stop looking for an easy way to get there.

There is no easy way to get to Jesus, just the right way. He will show you the right way if you seek Him first and listen to His voice. You can finish everything God has started in you if you go after it wholeheartedly, watch what comes out of your mouth, and guard your heart.

After hearing us preach this message the first time, our youngest son, Roman, said, "Daddy, that sounds like the saying, 'Any old dead fish can float downstream, but it takes a live one to swim upstream against the current!'"

Are you a dead fish floating downstream, or are you a live fish swimming upstream toward the finish line? Are you ready to accept Gabrielle's invitation to visit her heavenly home? Jesus is saying, "Come to Me. I am your destiny. Come to Me." If you want to swim toward your destiny and not be distracted any longer, pray this prayer:

Lord, I'm coming to You. I will not be distracted from my destiny anymore. I will not get off track. I'm headed toward You. I give You my heart and my commitment to do what You've called me to do and to keep my eyes focused on You. I won't be distracted by people, time, an offended heart, double-mindedness, fear, lack of direction, or the comparison trap. Heal any wounds I have been carrying in my heart. Forgive me for holding bitterness toward anyone or for not being obedient to Your call. I give You 100 percent of me. I'm all Yours, Lord. In Jesus' name, I'm coming to You.

We stand in agreement with you that you will fulfill your destiny in Christ and find His peace and happiness. Focus on what God has placed in your heart to do. Believe in what you are doing, and trust Him to make it all possible. Rip off the rearview mirror, and expand your vision above and beyond anything you have ever imagined. Nothing is impossible with God. He has called you to greatness, equipped you to overcome every distraction, and made provision for every need. Guard your assets, and run toward your destiny. Jesus is waiting.

ENDNOTES

Introduction

¹ Strong, "Hebrew," entry #2374, p. 28.

Chapter 1

¹ Strong, "Greek," entry #264, p. 10.

Chapter 4

¹ Marshall, p. 347.

Chapter 7

¹ Strong, "Hebrew," entry #2342, p. 38.

Chapter 9

¹ Roosevelt, Franklin D., *Inaugural Addresses of the Presidents of the United States.* Washington, D.C.: U.S. G.P.O.: for sale by the Supt. Of Docs., U.S. G.P.O., 1989; Bartleby.com, 2001.www.bartlby.com/124/.09/05/01.

References

Marshall, Catherine. *The Cherished Writings of Catherine Marshall.* Grand Rapids, Michigan: Family Christian Press.

Strong, James. *Strong's Exhaustive Concordance of the Bible, "Hebrew and Chaldee Dictionary," "Greek Dictionary of the New Testament."* Nashville: Abingdon, 1890.

About the Authors

Harry Salem II joined the Oral Roberts Ministry in 1980 and at the age of twenty-six became vice president of operations. In his work as author, television writer, producer, and director he has won several Angel and Addy Awards and has written the successful book *For Men Only*.

Cheryl Salem grew up in Choctaw County, Mississippi, and overcame many challenges to become Miss America 1980. She is an accomplished author, speaker, musician, recording artist, and teacher. She has recorded numerous albums and CDs and has written many best-selling books, including her autobiography, *A Bright Shining Place,* and most recently, *The Mommy Book.* She continues to co-host the popular national daily television program *Make Your Day Count.*

Salem Family Ministries focuses on family and restoration. They stress the unity of family, marriage, personal relationships, financial goals, and parenting. They also lead motivational meetings, men's conferences, and ladies' conferences on overcoming obstacles, such as abuse, abandonment, poor self-image, and financial difficulty.

Together Harry and Cheryl have written over sixteen books, including *An Angel's Touch* (a top-25 bestseller), *It's Too Soon To Give Up, Being #1 at Being #2, Speak the Word Over Your Family for Salvation, Speak the Word Over Your Family for Healing, Speak the Word Over Your Finances,* and their most powerful release, *From Mourning to Morning.*

When not at home in Tulsa, Oklahoma, the Salems continue to minister full-time throughout the world. Harry and Cheryl have three children, Harry III, Roman Lee, and Gabrielle Christian.

To contact Harry and Cheryl Salem
write:

Salem Family Ministries

P.O. Box 701287

Tulsa, Oklahoma 74170

Or visit their Web site:

www.salemfamilyministries.org

Please include your prayer requests
and comments when you write.

OTHER BOOKS BY
HARRY AND CHERYL SALEM

A Bright Shining Place

Abuse...Bruised but Not Broken

From Mourning to Morning

An Angel's Touch

For Men Only

Being #1 at Being #2

It's Too Soon To Give Up!

A Royal Child

The Mommy Book

You Are Somebody

A Fight in the Heavenlies (for children)

Warriors of the Word (for children)

Speak the Word Over Your Family for Salvation

Speak the Word Over Your Family for Healing

Speak the Word Over Your Family for Finances

Additional copies of this book and other book titles
from **Harrison House** are
available at your local bookstore.

Harrison House
Tulsa, Oklahoma 74153

THE HARRISON HOUSE VISION

Proclaiming the truth and the power

Of the Gospel of Jesus Christ

With excellence;

Challenging Christians to

Live victoriously,

Grow spiritually,

Know God intimately.